Building DeepSeek AI Models

Architecture, Implementation, and Optimization

X.Y. WANG

Disclaimer

This book has been authored with the assistance of LLM tools that supported the writing, editing, and formatting processes. Every effort has been made to ensure the content is accurate and of high quality. Readers are encouraged to engage critically with the material and verify information when necessary.

Contents

Preface

The rapid evolution of large language models (LLMs) has profoundly reshaped artificial intelligence research and application. Within this transformative landscape, DeepSeek has emerged as a notable force, delivering not only cutting-edge models but also embracing a philosophy of openness and collaboration. The release of DeepSeeks family of modelsranging from DeepSeek-V3 to the reasoning-focused DeepSeek-R1has provided researchers, developers, and practitioners with unprecedented opportunities to study, improve upon, and apply state-of-the-art language models without the constraints of closed ecosystems.

This book is written for readers who want to understand, replicate, and potentially extend the techniques used to build these influential models. It is neither a high-level survey nor a theoretical exploration of language modeling in general, but rather a focused and technically detailed guide to the practical methodologies underlying the DeepSeek models. By systematically unpacking DeepSeeks approaches to pre-training data curation, architecture design, training pipeline engineering, and evaluation strategies, the book aims to provide a clear and reproducible pathway for those who wish to replicate these techniques within their own projects.

Importantly, this book is not authored by the DeepSeek team, nor does it have any formal affiliation with DeepSeek. All content is derived from publicly available papers, code releases, benchmark results, and materials found in open-source repositories and the broader research literature. While every effort has been made to maintain accuracy and clarity, any errors or misinterpretations are solely the responsibility of the author.

The spirit of this book aligns closely with the ethos of open-source AI: to lower barriers to knowledge, foster collaborative learning, and accelerate progress through transparency. In that spirit, readers are encouraged not only to study the contents of this book, but to challenge, refine, and improve upon the techniques presented here. The ultimate goal is not simply to replicate existing work, but to empower researchers and engineers to push the field forwarddeveloping new models, improving efficiency, and broadening the application of advanced AI techniques.

The author hopes that this book will serve as both a practical guide and a source of inspiration for AI researchers, developers, and technology leaders who are passionate about open, reproducible, and responsible advancement of language model technology.

Let this be both a map and an invitationto explore, to learn, and to contribute to the future of open AI.

2

Chapter 1

Introduction

This chapter introduces DeepSeek and its family of language models, outlining their development and positioning within the broader landscape of open-source AI. It highlights the motivations behind these releases and their technical significance, particularly in the areas of reasoning and efficiency. The chapter also examines the broader impacts of DeepSeeks open-source strategy, including its influence on the research community and industry adoption.

1.1 Overview of DeepSeek and its AI Models

DeepSeek has rapidly ascended to become a prominent and influential entity in contemporary artificial intelligence research, particularly within the dynamic field of large language models (LLMs). Founded in July 2023 amidst a period of significant global technological evolution and evolving computational paradigms, DeepSeeks trajectory is a compelling narrative of technical innovation interwoven with the challenges of navigating geopolitical and resource-based constraints. This section provides a historical and contextual backdrop to the emergence of DeepSeeks pioneering models, establishing a foundational understanding before progressing to the detailed technical explorations in subsequent chapters.

The conceptual origins of DeepSeek can be traced to an era characterized by the rapid proliferation of deep learning methodologies and an escalating demand for AI systems adept at natural language understanding and generation.

The early 2010s marked a transformative phase in AI research, as neural network architectures began to demonstrably outperform traditional techniques across diverse applications, ranging from sophisticated image recognition to nuanced language translation. The advent of transformer models marked a pivotal moment, revolutionizing the natural language processing (NLP) landscape and establishing new performance benchmarks.

During this transformative period, numerous pioneering organizations and research institutions embarked on explorations into the potential of model scaling. However, this pursuit of scale was accompanied by substantial escalations in both computational expenditure and energy consumption. Concurrently, geopolitical factors, notably trade restrictions and constrained access to advanced semiconductor technologies, particularly high-performance GPUs, began to exert a considerable influence on the trajectory of AI research. These multifaceted challenges fostered a unique environment where the development of large-scale models necessitated innovative strategies to mitigate unsustainable cost implications.

It was within this complex and evolving environment that DeepSeek was established. Founded in July 2023 by Liang Wenfeng—an entrepreneur with a visionary approach and extensive experience in AI-driven financial trading—the company was conceived from a recognized need for efficient and economically viable AI solutions. DeepSeek's genesis was intrinsically linked to its parent hedge fund, which had already effectively harnessed the capabilities of GPU-accelerated deep learning for real-time, high-stakes decision-making within financial markets since 2016. This strategic pivot from algorithmic trading towards broader AI research was motivated by the realization that the methodologies refined in the demanding context of financial trading—particularly those emphasizing rapid data processing and resource optimization—could be effectively adapted to address wider challenges in natural language processing.

DeepSeek s foundational experience in the financial sector profoundly shaped its approach to model development. The high-pressure milieu of stock trading, where decision-making must occur in sub-second intervals, necessitates the ability to efficiently process and analyze vast datasets. DeepSeeks early systems effectively utilized GPU clusters to discern market trends and execute trades based on sophisticated deep learning models. These initial endeavors provided invaluable insights into the scalability of neural network architectures and the critical importance of resource optimization—lessons that would become foundational to the development of its advanced LLMs.

4

As DeepSeek strategically shifted its primary focus from financial algorithms to general-purpose language models, it retained a core philosophy of efficiency and innovation. The challenges posed by restricted access to advanced hardware, compounded by international limitations on cutting-edge chipsets, necessitated a departure from conventional model training paradigms. DeepSeeks team of engineers and researchers were thus compelled to re-evaluate traditional architectures and explore novel training methodologies. This strategic imperative aimed to facilitate the development of large-scale models without a commensurate and unsustainable increase in computational demands.

Technological and Industrial Influences

The period preceding DeepSeeks establishment was characterized by significant technological advancements and industrial shifts. The AI research community celebrated breakthroughs such as transformer architectures and self-supervised learning techniques, which empowered models to learn from expansive unstructured datasets. Simultaneously, leading industry entities were confronting the practical challenges of scaling these models to unprecedented dimensions. The inherent trade-offs between model size, training expenditures, and inference velocity became a central point of discussion and strategic consideration.

Within this dynamic landscape, DeepSeek strategically positioned itself as a disruptive innovator. Rather than directly competing with established organizations possessing substantial resources, DeepSeek adopted a strategic approach of doing more with less. By prioritizing efficiency and pioneering innovative architectures, the company aimed to develop models capable of achieving performance levels comparable to larger, more resource-intensive systems, while concurrently managing training costs effectively. This strategic orientation not only enabled DeepSeek to navigate the hardware constraints imposed by global supply chain complexities but also to pioneer novel methodologies that would subsequently influence the broader AI research community.

Key Milestones in the Development of DeepSeek Models

Since its inception in July 2023, DeepSeek has achieved a series of significant milestones that underscore its rapid advancement within the field of AI research. These milestones not only mark critical points of technical progress but also exemplify the companys dedication to transparency and collaborative engagement with the wider research community.

5

Early Experiments and Proof of Concept

Prior to the public unveiling of its advanced language models, DeepSeek made substantial investments in exploratory research initiatives. Initial experiments were focused on adapting existing transformer architectures to operate effectively within the limitations imposed by restricted hardware availability. Researchers investigated techniques such as parameter sharing, dynamic routing, and selective activation of network components. These foundational studies provided the essential groundwork for the adoption of the Mixture-of-Experts (MoE) approach—a pivotal architectural element in DeepSeeks model design. The MoE strategy enabled the company to achieve significant model scaling while effectively managing inference costs.

Public Model Releases and Evolution

DeepSeek s first major release, **DeepSeek -Coder** (January 2024), introduced code-specialized models trained on 2 trillion tokens across 87 programming languages. This established DeepSeeks credentials as a leader in code intelligence, directly competing with proprietary offerings like Codex. By June 2024, **DeepSeek -Coder-V2** expanded this work with a 236 billion parameter Mixture-of-Experts model, increasing language coverage to 338 programming languages and integrating strong mathematical reasoning capabilities.

In December 2024, **DeepSeek -V3** marked DeepSeeks entry into general-purpose LLM development. This 671 billion parameter MoE model, trained on 14.8 trillion tokens, introduced innovations such as *Multi-Token Prediction* and *Multi-Head Latent Attention*, extending its effective context length to 128K tokens while maintaining efficiency.

January 2025 saw the launch of **DeepSeek -R1**, a reasoning-optimized model trained via large-scale reinforcement learning (RL) using Group Relative Policy Optimization (GRPO). With superior performance in mathematical reasoning (solving 79.8% of AIME 2024 problems) and competitive programming tasks, DeepSeek-R1 demonstrated that advanced reasoning abilities could emerge directly from well-targeted RL incentives.

Distillation for Accessibility

To make these breakthroughs broadly accessible, DeepSeek subsequently distilled DeepSeek-R1 into smaller models, ranging from 1.5 billion to 70 billion parameters. These distilled models retained exceptional reasoning strength, outperforming all comparable open-source models in both reasoning and code

6

generation benchmarks.

Ongoing Commitment to Efficiency and Transparency

Throughout these milestones, DeepSeek consistently upheld its foundational philosophy: scale wisely, prioritize efficiency, and remain transparent. Each major release has been accompanied by open-weight model distributions, detailed technical reports, and collaborative benchmarking efforts. This commitment to openness has not only accelerated community adoption but also reinforced DeepSeeks reputation as a responsible company in AI development.

1.2 Impacts of DeepSeek's Model Releases

The introduction of DeepSeek's AI models has had profound and multifaceted effects across technological, economic, and geopolitical domains. This section examines these impacts, highlighting the responses from industry stakeholders, market dynamics, and international relations.

Technological Disruption and Industry Response: DeepSeek's release of cost-effective, open-source AI models has challenged traditional AI development paradigms. By demonstrating that high-performance AI can be achieved without extensive computational resources, DeepSeek has prompted industry leaders to reassess their strategies. Notably, advanced reasoning models like DeepSeek's R1 require significantly more computational power, underscoring the escalating demand for high-performance computing in AI applications.

Market Volatility and Economic Repercussions: The launch of DeepSeek's models, particularly the R1 chatbot, triggered substantial market reactions. Major technology companies experienced notable stock declines; for instance, Nvidia's shares dropped by approximately 17% following the release, marking a significant loss in market capitalization. This selloff extended to other tech giants, reflecting investor sensitivity to advancements in AI technology and the potential for disruptive innovation.

Geopolitical Tensions and Strategic Responses: DeepSeek's advancements have intensified geopolitical considerations, particularly concerning U.S.-China technological competition. The Chinese government has advised its AI experts to avoid traveling to the United States due to security concerns, reflecting apprehensions about safeguarding technological advancements and intellectual property. This development underscores the strategic importance of AI in national security and international relations.

Industry Adaptations and Strategic Shifts: In response to DeepSeek's innovations, companies like Microsoft have reevaluated their infrastructure investments. Reports indicate that Microsoft canceled leases on large data centers, reflecting concerns about potential oversupply and the implications of DeepSeek's cost-effective models on massive AI expenditures. Despite these adjustments, Microsoft maintains a commitment to substantial infrastructure spending, indicating a strategic reassessment rather than a reduction in AI ambitions.

Collaborative Potential and Open-Source Dynamics: DeepSeek's open-source approach has fostered discussions about global collaboration in AI development. By making its model weights freely accessible, DeepSeek has enabled a broader range of stakeholders to benefit from advanced AI technologies, potentially accelerating innovation and application across various sectors. This strategy contrasts with proprietary models and highlights the potential of open-source frameworks to democratize access to cutting-edge AI tools.

Investor Sentiment and Future Outlook: The emergence of DeepSeek has prompted analysts to reassess the AI investment landscape. While initial reactions included significant selloffs, some experts suggest that DeepSeek's advancements could ultimately benefit the broader AI market by spurring competition and innovation. For instance, companies like Nvidia may see increased demand for their high-performance computing products as AI applications become more sophisticated.

National Initiatives and Policy Implications: The success of DeepSeek has been perceived as a challenge to the global dominance of American AI initiatives. This development has prompted discussions at the highest levels of government, with U.S. leadership acknowledging the need for accelerated AI development to maintain technological leadership. Such acknowledgments may lead to increased funding for AI research and development, as well as the formulation of policies aimed at fostering innovation and addressing competitive pressures.

DeepSeek 's model releases have acted as a catalyst for significant shifts in the AI landscape, influencing technological strategies, market dynamics, geopolitical relations, and industry practices. The ripple effects of these developments continue to shape the trajectory of artificial intelligence on a global scale.

8

Chapter 2

Fundamentals of Large Language Models

This chapter covers the essential deep learning techniques required to build large language models, focusing on the transformer architecture, pre-training methods, and distributed training infrastructure. It explains how self-supervised pre-training, attention mechanisms, and optimization techniques work together to scale language models effectively. Finally, it introduces the core evaluation metrics used to assess model performance during and after training.

2.1 Transformer Architecture

The transformer architecture has become the backbone of modern natural language processing and large language models such as DeepSeek. By replacing sequential models like recurrent neural networks (RNNs) and long short-term memory networks (LSTMs) with a mechanism that processes all tokens simultaneously, transformers have enabled significant improvements in both training efficiency and performance.

Traditional sequence models process input one token at a time, which can hinder the models ability to capture long-range dependencies and slow down training considerably. The transformer architecture was introduced to address these limitations. Instead of processing tokens sequentially, transformers use a self-attention mechanism that allows every token in a sequence to interact with every other token concurrently. This parallel processing not only accelerates training but also improves the models capacity to learn relationships over long distances in text.

Tokenization and Embeddings

Before any model can process text, the raw data must be converted into a numerical format. This transformation occurs in two steps: tokenization and embedding.

Tokenization is the process of breaking down raw text into smaller units called tokens. Tokens may represent words, subwords, or even characters. DeepSeek and many other modern language models typically employ subword tokenization methodssuch as Byte-Pair Encoding (BPE) or SentencePiecebecause these techniques provide a balanced approach. Common words can be treated as single tokens, while less frequent or compound words are split into smaller, meaningful pieces. For example, the word "unbelievable" might be tokenized into "un", "believ", and "able." This not only reduces the overall vocabulary size but also improves the models ability to generalize from known subcomponents.

Once tokenization is complete, each token must be converted into a high-dimensional vector, a process called embedding. Suppose the vocabulary contains V tokens, and each token is represented by a vector of dimension d. The embedding matrix E is of size $V \times d$, where each row corresponds to a tokens vector representation. For any token t, its embedding is given by

$$\mathbf{x}_t = E[t].$$

This equation indicates that each token t is mapped to a vector $\mathbf{x}_t$ from the matrix E. These embeddings capture semantic relationships between tokens and serve as the foundation for all subsequent computations in the transformer.

Positional Encodings

In a transformer, tokens are processed in parallel rather than one-by-one, which means the model does not naturally know the order of the tokens. Positional encodings provide a way to inject this order information into the model by adding a unique, position-dependent vector to each token's embedding.

Consider reading a sentence with its words in a random orderthe meaning

10

would be lost because grammar and syntax depend on word order. Positional encodings ensure that each token's position in the sequence is taken into account.

A widely used method for creating positional encodings is based on sinusoidal functions. In the original transformer model, the positional encoding for a token at position *pos* is defined by the following equations:

$$PE_{(pos,2i)} = \sin\left(\frac{pos}{10000^{\frac{2i}{d}}}\right), \quad PE_{(pos,2i+1)} = \cos\left(\frac{pos}{10000^{\frac{2i}{d}}}\right).$$

Here is what each component means:

- *pos*: This is the position of the token in the sequence (starting from 0 or 1).

- *i*: This is the index of the dimension within the positional encoding vector.

- *d*: This represents the dimensionality of the token embeddings, meaning the length of the vector that represents each token. For example, if $d = 512$, each token is represented by a 512-dimensional vector.

- Sine and Cosine Functions:

  - The sine function is applied to the even-indexed dimensions (0, 2, 4, ...).

  - The cosine function is applied to the odd-indexed dimensions (1, 3, 5, ...).

- Scaling Factor $10000^{\frac{2i}{d}}$: This factor scales the position *pos* so that different dimensions capture information at different frequencies. Lower dimensions correspond to higher frequencies (capturing fine-grained positional differences), while higher dimensions correspond to lower frequencies (capturing broader positional trends).

By adding these sinusoidal positional encodings to the token embeddings

$$\mathbf{z}_t = \mathbf{x}_t + \mathbf{p}_t,$$

11

each token's final representation, $\mathbf{z}_t$, carries both its semantic information (from $\mathbf{x}_t$) and its position within the sequence (from $\mathbf{p}_t$). This combined information allows the transformer to effectively understand and process the order of words, which is critical for tasks like translation, summarization, and text generation.

The final input representation for a token is the sum of its embedding and its positional encoding:

$$\mathbf{z}_t = \mathbf{x}_t + \mathbf{p}_t.$$

This simple additive combination means that each tokens vector now carries both its semantic meaning (from the embedding) and its positional context (from the positional encoding).

Self-Attention Mechanism

The self-attention mechanism is a central component of the transformer architecture that enables the model to dynamically capture dependencies between tokens in a sequence. Unlike traditional models that process tokens sequentially, self-attention allows each token to attend to all other tokens simultaneously, assigning different weights based on their relevance. Below is an expanded explanation of this process.

1. Projection into Queries, Keys, and Values

For each token in the input sequence, the model generates three distinct vectors: the query (Q), the key (K), and the value (V). Suppose we have an input matrix X of shape $N \times d$, where

- N is the number of tokens in the sequence.
- d is the embedding dimension (i.e., the length of each token's vector).

To compute Q, K, and V, the input X is multiplied by three different weight matrices, which are learned during training:

$$Q = XW^Q, \quad K = XW^K, \quad V = XW^V.$$

- W^Q, W^K, and W^V: These are the learned weight matrices. They transform the original embeddings into new spaces where the self-attention mechanism can operate effectively.

12

- Query (Q) Vector: For a given token, the query vector represents what information it is seeking from the rest of the sequence.

- Key (K) Vector: The key vector of a token represents its content in a way that allows it to be matched with queries from other tokens.

- Value (V) Vector: The value vector contains the actual information of the token that will be aggregated based on the computed attention scores.

For example, if token i is represented by $\mathbf{x}_i$ in X, then

$$\mathbf{q}_i = \mathbf{x}_i W^Q, \quad \mathbf{k}_i = \mathbf{x}_i W^K, \quad \mathbf{v}_i = \mathbf{x}_i W^V.$$

This step lays the groundwork for comparing tokens with one another in the next stages.

2. Calculating Attention Scores

Once we have Q, K, and V for all tokens, the next step is to calculate how much attention each token should pay to every other token. This is done by computing the dot product between the query vector of one token and the key vectors of all tokens.

For tokens i and j, the unscaled attention score is given by

$$\text{Score}(i, j) = \mathbf{q}_i \cdot \mathbf{k}_j.$$

However, these dot products can result in large numbers, especially when the dimensionality d (or more precisely, d_k the dimension of the key vectors) is high. To control the scale and help stabilize the gradients during training, the score is divided by the square root of d_k:

$$\text{Scaled Score}(i, j) = \frac{\mathbf{q}_i \cdot \mathbf{k}_j}{\sqrt{d_k}}.$$

Here,

- d_k: This is the dimensionality of the key vectors. Often in practice, d_k is set equal to d or is a fraction of d when using multi-head attention.

Scaling helps prevent the softmax function (applied in the next step) from having extremely small gradients when the scores are large.

3. Softmax and Weighted Sum

To convert the scaled scores into a probability distribution that indicates how much attention each token should receive, the softmax function is applied to each set of scores:

$$\alpha_{ij} = \text{softmax}\left(\frac{\mathbf{q}_i \cdot \mathbf{k}_j}{\sqrt{d_k}}\right).$$

This operation is applied row-wise, meaning for each token i, the softmax produces a set of weights $\{\alpha_{i1}, \alpha_{i2}, \ldots, \alpha_{iN}\}$ that sum to 1. These weights indicate the relevance of each token j to token i.

Finally, these attention weights are used to compute a weighted sum of the value vectors V:

$$\text{Attention}(Q, K, V) = \text{softmax}\left(\frac{QK^T}{\sqrt{d_k}}\right)V.$$

Here,

- QK^T: This matrix multiplication computes the dot product between each query and each key, resulting in a matrix of scores.

- $\frac{QK^T}{\sqrt{d_k}}$: The scaling is applied element-wise to ensure the values remain manageable.

- softmax $\left(\frac{QK^T}{\sqrt{d_k}}\right)$: Softmax is applied to each row, turning the scores into attention weights.

- Multiplying by V: The attention weights are used to take a weighted sum of the value vectors, resulting in a new representation for each token that is enriched with contextual information from the entire sequence.

This weighted sum allows each token to integrate information from all other tokens, with the contribution of each token modulated by how relevant it is to the current token.

To recap:

14

1. **Projection:** Each token's embedding is transformed into query, key, and value vectors using learned matrices.

2. **Score Calculation:** The dot product between the query and key vectors determines the relevance of tokens, and the scores are scaled to keep values stable.

3. **Normalization and Aggregation:** The softmax function converts these scores into a probability distribution, which is then used to compute a weighted sum of the value vectors. This produces a contextually enriched representation for each token.

The self-attention mechanism, by allowing each token to consider every other token in the sequence, is what empowers transformers to capture complex, long-range dependencies in language. This dynamic process of attending to different parts of the input is a key reason why transformer-based models like DeepSeek have achieved such remarkable success in various natural language processing tasks.

Multi-Head Attention

Multi-head attention builds upon the self-attention mechanism by allowing the model to capture different aspects of relationships between tokens simultaneously. Instead of performing a single self-attention calculation on the entire input, the input is split into several heads, with each head processing a distinct portion of the embedding. This design enables the model to attend to various features such as syntactic patterns, semantic meanings, or even positional nuances in parallel.

Lets break down the process:

1. *Splitting the Input into Multiple Heads:* The input matrix X (of shape $N \times d$, where N is the number of tokens and d is the embedding dimension) is first projected into three matricesqueries (Q), keys (K), and values (V)using learned weight matrices, just as in self-attention:

$$Q = XW^Q, \quad K = XW^K, \quad V = XW^V.$$

To create multiple heads, these projected matrices are split along the embedding dimension into h smaller matrices. Each head will then have dimensions $N \times \frac{d}{h}$.

15

2. *Independent Attention Computation per Head:* For each head i, the scaled dot-product attention is computed independently:

$$\text{head}_i = \text{Attention}(Q_i, K_i, V_i) = \text{softmax}\left(\frac{Q_i K_i^T}{\sqrt{d_k}}\right) V_i,$$

where Q_i, K_i, and V_i are the query, key, and value matrices for head i, and $d_k = \frac{d}{h}$ is the dimensionality of each heads key vectors. This independent computation allows each head to focus on different parts or patterns within the data.

3. *Concatenation and Final Projection:* The outputs from all heads are then concatenated along the feature dimension to form a single matrix:

$$\text{Concat}(\text{head}_1, \ldots, \text{head}_h).$$

This concatenated matrix is projected back to the original dimension d using a final weight matrix W^O:

$$\text{MultiHead}(X) = \text{Concat}(\text{head}_1, \ldots, \text{head}_h)W^O.$$

The final projection blends the information captured by each head into a unified representation that can be passed to subsequent layers.

Diagram: Multi-Head Attention

16

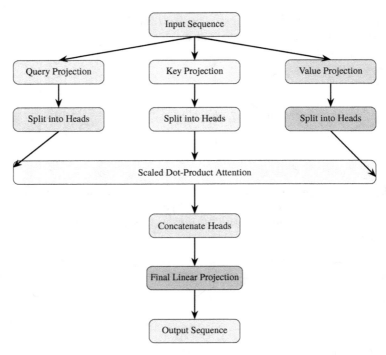

Figure 2.1: Multi-head attention: The input sequence is projected into queries, keys, and values, split into multiple heads, processed in parallel via scaled dot-product attention, concatenated, and finally projected back to the original dimensionality.

This diagram visually outlines the steps of multi-head attention, showing how the input is transformed into multiple attention outputs that are then merged into a single comprehensive representation.

Feedforward Networks and Residual Connections

After the multi-head attention layer, each transformer layer includes a feedforward network (FFN) and employs residual connections combined with layer normalization to further process the token representations and maintain stability during training.

Feedforward Network Structure

17

The feedforward network is applied to each token independently and is responsible for adding non-linearity to the model. It typically consists of two linear transformations with a non-linear activation function between them. The structure can be summarized by the following equation:

$$FFN(x) = ReLU(xW_1 + b_1)W_2 + b_2.$$

Here is what each component represents:

- x: The input vector for a token.

- W_1 and W_2: Learned weight matrices that transform the input.

- b_1 and b_2: Bias vectors that are added after each linear transformation.

- ReLU Activation: The Rectified Linear Unit (ReLU) introduces non-linearity, enabling the network to capture complex patterns.

This two-layer structure allows the network to transform the token representations into a richer, more abstract space, further enhancing the model's understanding of the data.

Residual Connections and Layer Normalization

Deep neural networks, including transformers, can suffer from issues like vanishing gradients, which make training difficult as the number of layers increases. Residual connections help address these problems by allowing the original input of a layer to be added directly to its output. This "skip connection" ensures that important information is preserved throughout the network and facilitates the flow of gradients during backpropagation.

For the multi-head attention sublayer, the output is combined with the original input using a residual connection and then normalized:

$$Y = LayerNorm(X + MultiHead(X)).$$

Similarly, after the feedforward network, the residual connection is applied:

$$Z = LayerNorm(Y + FFN(Y)).$$

In these equations:

- X: The input to the sublayer (either the output from the previous layer or the output of the multi-head attention).

- Y: The intermediate output after the multi-head attention and before the feedforward network.

- LayerNorm($\cdot$): Layer normalization, which scales and shifts the summed outputs to ensure that the data's distribution remains consistent throughout the network.

Layer normalization is critical because it stabilizes the learning process and allows for deeper networks without suffering from internal covariate shift.

Architectural Variants: Encoder-Decoder and Decoder-Only

Transformers can be adapted for different tasks by modifying their overall structure. Two common configurations are the encoder-decoder architecture and the decoder-only architecture.

Encoder-Decoder Architecture: The encoder-decoder model is used primarily for sequence-to-sequence tasks, such as machine translation. In this setup:

- Encoder: Processes the input sequence to produce a contextualized representation of each token.

- Decoder: Uses the encoder's output along with its own self-attention mechanism to generate the output sequence.

This architecture is effective because the encoder thoroughly understands the input, and the decoder leverages this information to produce relevant and coherent outputs.

Decoder-Only Architecture: For tasks like language modeling and text generation, a decoder-only architecture is typically used. In this configuration, the model predicts the next token in a sequence based solely on the tokens generated so far:

$$p(x_{t+1} \mid x_1, x_2, \ldots, x_t).$$

To prevent the model from accessing future tokens during training, a causal (or triangular) mask is applied. This mask sets the attention scores for future tokens to zero:

19

$$\mathbf{w}_{ij} = \begin{cases} 0 & \text{if } j > i, \\ \mathbf{w}_{ij} & \text{otherwise.} \end{cases}$$

This ensures that the prediction for token x_{t+1} depends only on the tokens x_1 to x_t, maintaining the autoregressive property of language modeling.

Together, multi-head attention, feedforward networks, residual connections, and careful architectural design form the backbone of transformer models. These components work in concert to enable transformers to learn rich, complex representations of language, making them highly effective for a variety of natural language processing tasks.

Bridging Theory and Practical Applications

While the mathematical formulations and architectural details provide a strong theoretical foundation, practical implementations of transformers—such as DeepSeek—require additional considerations.

Efficiency and Scalability: One of the main challenges with self-attention is its quadratic complexity with respect to sequence length. As the number of tokens increases, the computational resources required can become prohibitive. To address this, researchers have proposed several strategies:

- **Sparse Attention:** Limiting the attention mechanism to a subset of tokens to reduce computational load.

- **Low-Rank Approximations:** Approximating the attention matrices to lower the dimensionality.

- **Efficient Transformer Variants:** Architectures such as Longformer or Performer introduce modifications specifically designed to handle longer sequences without sacrificing performance.

Normalization and Stability: The use of layer normalization is critical for maintaining training stability. Some models experiment with alternative normalization strategies, such as pre-norm configurations (applying normalization before the sublayer) rather than post-norm. These choices can affect convergence speed and overall model performance, and are active areas of research.

Positional Encoding Alternatives: Although sinusoidal positional encodings are widely used due to their simplicity and deterministic nature, alternative approaches have emerged. For example, rotary positional embeddings (RoPE) integrate positional information in a way that can be more flexible and may offer performance benefits in certain contexts. Understanding these alternatives allows practitioners to make informed decisions based on the specific requirements of their application.

Real-World Applications of Transformers

Transformers have been applied successfully across a wide range of natural language processing tasks, demonstrating the versatility of the architecture:

- **Machine Translation:** Encoder-decoder transformers are highly effective at converting text from one language to another by first understanding the source language and then generating a fluent translation.

- **Text Summarization:** By leveraging long-range dependencies, transformers can produce coherent and concise summaries of long documents.

- **Chatbots and Conversational AI:** Decoder-only models, trained on large conversational datasets, are capable of generating contextually relevant and engaging responses.

- **Content Generation:** Whether it is creative writing or code generation, transformers have demonstrated a remarkable ability to generate humanlike text based on a given prompt.

The insights from transformer architectures have also led to the development of advanced techniques in transfer learning, where models pre-trained on vast corpora are fine-tuned for specific tasks with minimal additional training.

Transformers represent a significant evolution in the design of neural networks for natural language processing. By combining tokenization, embeddings, positional encodings, self-attention, multi-head attention, and feedforward networks with residual connections and normalization techniques, the transformer architecture provides a robust framework for understanding and generating language.

In summary:

- **Tokenization and Embeddings:** Convert raw text into meaningful vector representations.

- **Positional Encodings:** Integrate order information using deterministic functions.

- **Self-Attention:** Allow each token to dynamically weigh the influence of every other token in the sequence.

- **Multi-Head Attention:** Capture diverse relationships by processing multiple attention heads in parallel.

- **Feedforward Networks and Residual Connections:** Enhance feature representations and stabilize deep network training.

- **Architectural Variants:** Adapt the transformer design to tasks like translation (encoder-decoder) or language modeling (decoder-only) by appropriate modifications such as causal masking.

Understanding these components and their mathematical foundations not only demystifies how transformers work but also provides valuable insights into the practical challenges and solutions in modern natural language processing systems.

2.2 Pre-training Techniques

Pre-training is the phase during which large language models (LLMs) build a broad understanding of language, code, reasoning, and various types of textual data. Unlike supervised learning, where models learn from labeled examples, pre-training for language models uses *self-supervised learning*a method that creates training signals directly from the structure of the data itself. This explanation is designed to help intermediate-level readers understand not only the how but also the why behind these techniques.

Self-Supervised Pre-training. In self-supervised learning, the model is trained on raw text without any externally provided labels. Instead of relying on manually annotated data, the model generates its own training targets from the text. For example, by removing or masking parts of the text and asking the model to predict the missing pieces, the model learns to understand context, grammar, and semantics. This method allows the use of vast amounts of unannotated dataranging from books and websites to code repositories and scientific articleswhich is crucial for building models with general language competence.

22

The strength of self-supervised pre-training lies in its ability to scale. By processing billions of sentences, the model gradually internalizes not only basic language rules but also more subtle patterns such as reasoning structures, cultural references, and domain-specific knowledge. This broad base of learning then serves as a foundation when the model is later fine-tuned for specific tasks.

Causal Language Modeling (CLM). A common self-supervised objective for language models is **causal language modeling (CLM)**. In CLM, the model is trained to predict each token in a sequence based only on the tokens that precede it. Mathematically, the training objective is to maximize the probability:

$$\prod_{t=1}^{T} p(x_t \mid x_1, x_2, \ldots, x_{t-1})$$

This formulation enforces a strict left-to-right order, similar to how we naturally write and read text. During training, the model sees a sequence such as:

$$\text{Tokens: } [\text{The, cat, sat, on, the, mat}]$$

It then learns to predict each token from its preceding context:

$$p(\text{cat} \mid \text{The}), \quad p(\text{sat} \mid \text{The, cat}), \quad \ldots$$

To ensure that each token only sees its leftward context during training, a triangular attention mask is used. This mask restricts the models attention such that token x_t can only consider tokens x_1 through x_t (including itself), as illustrated below:

$$\begin{bmatrix} 1 & 0 & 0 & 0 & \ldots \\ 1 & 1 & 0 & 0 & \ldots \\ 1 & 1 & 1 & 0 & \ldots \\ \vdots & \vdots & \vdots & \ddots & \end{bmatrix}$$

This causal constraint not only ensures the model learns in a natural, sequential manner but also allows it to generate text coherently during inferencemimicking the process of writing.

Why CLM Matters. Causal language modeling is particularly effective for tasks that involve text generation. Whether it is writing code, composing emails, or generating creative stories, the autoregressive nature of CLM supports the step-by-step generation of coherent and contextually relevant text.

For models like DeepSeek-R1, this means that each new word is generated based solely on what has come before, allowing the model to maintain a logical and fluid narrative as it processes longer contexts.

Data Preparation: Composition, Cleaning, and Formatting. Even the most advanced training algorithms cannot compensate for poor data quality. The pre-training data must be diverse, high-quality, and carefully curated to provide the model with a rich learning experience.

Data Composition. A robust pre-training corpus is assembled from a variety of sources. Typical components include:

- **Web Text:** Data from Wikipedia, news sites, forums, and blogs.

- **Books:** Both public domain and licensed collections that cover a wide range of topics.

- **Code Repositories:** Open-source projects from platforms like GitHub.

- **Scientific Papers:** Technical reports, preprints from ArXiv or PubMed.

- **Instructional Text:** Tutorials, documentation, and other forms of educational material.

The diversity of the data ensures that the model learns not only the general structure of language but also domain-specific knowledgevital for tasks like code generation and technical problem-solving.

Data Cleaning and Deduplication. Raw data collected from the web is often noisy and redundant. Inaccuracies, spam, and duplicate content can harm the models ability to generalize. Therefore, several cleaning techniques are applied:

- **Duplicate Removal:** Techniques like minhash and Jaccard similarity are used to detect and remove near-duplicate documents. This prevents the model from overfitting to redundant content.

- **Spam and Boilerplate Filtering:** Irrelevant or low-quality textsuch as spam, advertisement content, or boilerplate languageis filtered out.

- **Exclusion of Machine-Generated Text:** Text generated by previous language models is removed to avoid reinforcing any existing biases or errors.

24

- **Language and Domain Filtering:** Ensuring a balanced representation of languages and topics so that the model does not become overly biased toward any single domain.

These steps are crucial because even small amounts of poor-quality data can mislead the model during training, resulting in degraded performance on real-world tasks.

Document Formatting and Chunking. After cleaning, the data must be structured in a way that is compatible with the models architecture. Transformers typically work with fixed-length input sequences (e.g., 2048 tokens). Therefore, long documents must be split into smaller, coherent chunks. However, arbitrary splitting can break the context and flow of the text. Instead, careful chunking is performed:

- **Preserving Coherence:** Chunks are preferably split at natural boundaries, such as paragraph breaks, section headings, or logical transitions in the text.

- **Special Considerations for Code:** For code repositories, it is important to maintain file boundaries, function definitions, and logical code blocks to preserve the structural integrity of the code.

Proper formatting and chunking ensure that each training example is both coherent and contextually complete, allowing the model to learn effective representations.

Pre-training Pipeline Overview. The pre-training process can be visualized as a sequential pipeline, where each step is vital for the final model quality:

Figure 2.2: Simplified pre-training pipeline for language models

- **Raw Data Collection:** The process starts with gathering vast amounts of data from diverse sources.

- **Cleaning & Deduplication:** Next, the data is rigorously cleaned to remove duplicates, spam, and low-quality content.

- **Document Formatting & Chunking:** The cleaned data is then formatted into consistent, coherent chunks that the model can efficiently process.

- **Tokenization:** The formatted text is converted into tokenssmaller units of text that serve as the models input.

- **CLM Training:** The model is trained using causal language modeling, where it learns to predict the next token in a sequence based on the previous tokens.

- **Perplexity Evaluation:** Finally, the models performance is evaluated using metrics like perplexity, which measures how well the model predicts a sample.

The Scale and Impact of Pre-training. Modern language models are trained on trillions of tokens, enabling them to capture rare linguistic phenomena, idiomatic expressions, and domain-specific knowledge. For instance, GPT-4 is estimated to have been trained on over 10 trillion tokens, covering a broad spectrum of publicly available text. This vast training scale allows models to perform impressively across many languages and domains, from code generation to creative writing and technical problem-solving.

Pre-training is the critical phase that defines what the model knows. While the architecture provides the potential to express complex ideas, the quality, diversity, and scale of the pre-training data determine the depth and breadth of that knowledge. By combining self-supervised learning with effective data curation and causal language modeling, developers create models that serve as versatile foundations for a wide range of downstream tasks.

Pre-training techniques enable LLMs to develop a deep, general understanding of language without the need for manual labeling. By carefully assembling and cleaning vast amounts of data, formatting it for coherent input, and using causal language modeling to guide learning, these models gain the ability to perform complex language tasks. This foundation is essential not only for generating fluent and coherent text but also for fine-tuning models for specialized applications in various domains.

2.3 Basic Training Infrastructure

Training large language models like DeepSeek-R1 requires infrastructure far beyond a single machine or even a single data center server. The sheer size of these modelstens to hundreds of billions of parameterscombined with the trillions of tokens needed for effective pre-training makes efficient distributed training across clusters of GPUs essential. This section explains the basic training infrastructure that underpins such efforts, including distributed training strategies, parallelism techniques, and the critical role of mixed-precision arithmetic in making training feasible.

Why Distributed Training is Necessary.

The memory requirements for training large transformers exceed what can fit on a single GPU. Even if all parameters fit into memory, the need to process large batches for statistical efficiency, coupled with high-resolution gradients, makes distributed training inevitable. For example, a 70-billion parameter model requires around 140GB of memory just to store the weights in FP32far beyond the memory of any single GPU.

Additionally, training times must be kept reasonable. Training a trillion-token corpus on a single machine could take years. Splitting the load across hundreds or thousands of GPUs reduces training time to weeks or months. This combination of model size and data volume necessitates a sophisticated **distributed training infrastructure**.

The Three Dimensions of Parallelism

Modern distributed training relies on **three complementary forms of parallelism**, each addressing a different bottleneck:

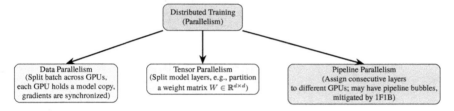

Figure 2.3: The Three Dimensions of Parallelism

- **Data Parallelism**. In data parallelism, the training batch is split across multiple GPUs. Each GPU processes a different slice of data using its own copy of the model. After processing, gradients from all GPUs are averaged (synchronized), and the model is updated in unison. This is the simplest form of parallelism, but it does not address models too large to fit on a single GPU.

- **Tensor Parallelism**. Tensor parallelism splits the layers themselves across devices. For example, each matrix multiplication might be split so that each GPU holds only part of the weight matrix. This allows extremely large models to fit across multiple GPUs.

  If the weight matrix for a layer is $W \in \mathbb{R}^{d \times d}$ and there are four GPUs, each GPU might store a quarter-sized shard W_1, W_2, W_3, W_4. During forward and backward passes, GPUs collectively compute the full matrix multiplication using efficient communication (all-reduce or all-gather).

- **Pipeline Parallelism**. In pipeline parallelism, consecutive layers are assigned to different GPUs. This allows the entire model to be split into stages, each handled by a subset of devices. For example, layers 1–12 might reside on GPU group 1, while layers 13–24 reside on GPU group 2.

  However, this introduces a pipeline bubble: the time during which early GPUs finish their work and must wait for later GPUs to catch up. Advanced pipeline strategies like **1F1B** (one forward, one backward pass overlapping) mitigate this problem.

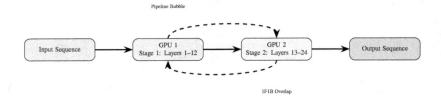

Figure 2.4: Pipeline Parallelism

Combining Parallelism Techniques

For massive models, none of these techniques suffices alone. Modern training combines all three:

- `Data parallelism` splits the batch across GPU nodes.

- `Tensor parallelism` splits each layer across GPUs within a node.

- `Pipeline parallelism` splits the model vertically across different nodes.

This hybrid approach ensures both memory efficiency and maximal hardware utilization. Below is a high-level summary table:

29

Parallelism	Splits	Purpose
Data Parallelism	Batch	Handle large data
Tensor Parallelism	Layer Matrix	Fit large layers
Pipeline Parallelism	Layers	Fit entire model

Table 2.1: Comparison of parallelism techniques

Communication Efficiency

All distributed training requires **communication** to synchronize gradients, share activations, or transfer intermediate results. Efficient communication libraries, such as NVIDIA NCCL, are crucial. Poorly optimized communication can bottleneck training, with GPUs spending more time waiting for data than computing gradients.

For example, data parallelism requires all GPUs to exchange gradients at the end of each batch. This is often done using an *all-reduce* operation:

$$\text{AllReduce}(g_i) = \frac{1}{N} \sum_{k=1}^{N} g_k$$

For tensor parallelism, the output of a matrix multiplication must be reconstructed by gathering partial results across GPUs:

$$Y = \text{MatMul}(X, [W_1, W_2, \dots]) \rightarrow \text{AllGather}(Y)$$

Effective overlap of computation and communication is key to maintaining high hardware utilization.

Mixed-Precision Training.

Another vital technique in large-scale training is **mixed-precision training**, which uses lower precision (e.g., FP16 or BF16) for most computations while retaining higher precision (e.g., FP32) for select accumulations, such as the master copy of model weights.

Mixed precision offers two primary benefits:

- **Memory savings**: Halving precision roughly halves memory use, allowing larger batches and models.

- **Speed**: Modern GPUs have specialized hardware (Tensor Cores) optimized for low-precision matrix math, greatly accelerating computation.

30

A typical mixed-precision training loop includes:

```
with torch.autocast("cuda"):
    loss = model(input).loss
scaler.scale(loss).backward()
scaler.step(optimizer)
scaler.update()
```

Here, the `autocast` context ensures forward pass operations use lower precision, while the gradient scaler handles dynamic adjustment of gradients to prevent underflow. This technique allows stable training even in reduced precision.

Hardware and Cluster Setup

State-of-the-art training runs typically require:

- Thousands of A100, H100, or similar GPUs.

- High-bandwidth interconnects like NVLink within nodes.

- RDMA-capable network fabric between nodes (e.g., InfiniBand).

- Large shared storage (e.g., Lustre or GPFS) for dataset access.

A representative cluster might look like:

Component	Example
GPU	NVIDIA H100
Per-node GPU count	8
Inter-node bandwidth	200 Gbps
Cluster size	2048 GPUs
Storage	Parallel file system

Table 2.2: Example cluster configuration for LLM training

Monitoring and Failure Recovery.

With thousands of GPUs working in tandem, hardware failures are inevitable. Modern training frameworks incorporate:

- Automatic checkpointing.

31

- Elastic recoveryrebalancing workloads after node failures.

- Real-time monitoring of utilization, communication overhead, and memory pressure.

Large language model training would be infeasible without a sophisticated combination of distributed parallelism, mixed-precision arithmetic, and high-performance hardware infrastructure. These foundational techniques form the operational backbone of every modern LLM project, enabling researchers to transform architectural innovations into practical, scalable models that can reason across vast domains of human knowledge.

2.4   Optimization Algorithms: Challenges and Solutions

Training large language models (LLMs) involves minimizing a loss function over billions of parameters using datasets that span trillions of tokens. This optimization problem is difficult for several reasons:

- **High Dimensionality:** The vast number of parameters creates a highly non-convex and rugged optimization landscape with many local minima and saddle points.

- **Noisy Gradients:** When using massive datasets, the gradients computed on mini-batches can be extremely noisy, which complicates convergence.

- **Memory Constraints:** Storing all intermediate activations for back-propagation in deep models is often impractical due to hardware limitations.

To address these challenges, modern LLM training pipelines incorporate a suite of techniques. In this section, we explain the problems and present the solutions that have been developed, covering adaptive optimization, dynamic learning rate scheduling, and memory efficiency strategies.

Adaptive Optimization with AdamW

Standard stochastic gradient descent (SGD) updates parameters uniformly:

$$\theta_{t+1} = \theta_t - \eta \, g_t,$$

where η is the learning rate and $g_t = \nabla_\theta \mathcal{L}(\theta_t)$ is the gradient at step t. However, when different parameters behave differently, using a single learning rate for all parameters can lead to slow convergence or instability.

Adam (Adaptive Moment Estimation) was designed to overcome these issues by adapting the learning rate on a per-parameter basis. It does this by maintaining:

- **First Moment (Mean) Estimate:**

$$m_t = \beta_1 m_{t-1} + (1 - \beta_1) g_t,$$

  which serves as a momentum term to smooth out noisy gradients.

- **Second Moment (Variance) Estimate:**

$$v_t = \beta_2 v_{t-1} + (1 - \beta_2) g_t^2.$$

Since both m_t and v_t start at zero, they are biased during the initial iterations. Bias-corrected estimates are computed as:

$$\hat{m}_t = \frac{m_t}{1 - \beta_1^t}, \quad \hat{v}_t = \frac{v_t}{1 - \beta_2^t}.$$

The update rule for Adam becomes:

$$\theta_{t+1} = \theta_t - \eta \frac{\hat{m}_t}{\sqrt{\hat{v}_t} + \epsilon},$$

where ϵ is a small constant to avoid division by zero.

Decoupling Weight Decay: AdamW In standard Adam, weight decay (L2 regularization) is applied directly to the gradients. However, this can interfere with the adaptive scaling of gradients. AdamW addresses this by decoupling weight decay from the gradient update. After computing the Adam update, weight decay is applied directly:

$$\theta_{t+1} = \theta_t - \eta \frac{\hat{m}_t}{\sqrt{\hat{v}_t} + \epsilon} - \eta \lambda \theta_t,$$

where λ is the weight decay coefficient. This decoupling ensures that weight decay acts as a true regularizer without distorting the adaptive updates.

Practical Settings for AdamW For training LLMs, typical AdamW hyperparameters might be:

Parameter	Typical Value
Learning rate (peak)	1×10^{-4}
β_1	0.9
β_2	0.95
Weight decay (λ)	0.1
ϵ	1×10^{-8}

Table 2.3: Typical AdamW hyperparameters for transformer pre-training

Dynamic Learning Rate Scheduling: Warmup and Cosine Decay

Using a fixed learning rate throughout training is rarely effective. Early in training, when the models parameters are far from optimal, a high learning rate can lead to unstable updates. Later, as the model begins to converge, a high learning rate may prevent fine-tuning of the parameters.

Learning Rate Warmup

The warmup phase gradually increases the learning rate from a very low value to a peak value over T_{warmup} steps:

$$\eta_t = \eta_{\max} \frac{t}{T_{\text{warmup}}}, \quad \text{for } t \leq T_{\text{warmup}}.$$

This prevents large, unstable updates at the start of training.

Cosine Decay

Once the model has warmed up, the learning rate is gradually decreased using a cosine decay schedule:

$$\eta_t = \eta_{\min} + \frac{1}{2}(\eta_{\max} - \eta_{\min})\left(1 + \cos\left(\frac{t - T_{\text{warmup}}}{T_{\text{total}} - T_{\text{warmup}}}\pi\right)\right).$$

Here, $\eta_{\min}$ is the minimum learning rate and T_{total} is the total number of training steps. This schedule enables large updates initially and progressively smaller, fine-tuning updates as training converges.

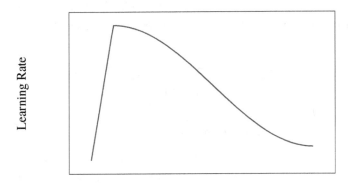

Training Steps

Figure 2.5: Example of a learning rate schedule combining warmup (first 10 steps) and cosine decay (remaining steps)

Memory Efficiency Techniques

Training deep and wide models not only requires a lot of computation but also a significant amount of memory to store intermediate activations during the forward pass. This can be a limiting factor when training on available hardware.

Gradient checkpointing reduces memory usage by saving only a subset of intermediate activations during the forward pass. When these activations are needed for backpropagation, they are recomputed on the fly. Although this increases computation time, it can reduce memory consumption by 3050%. In PyTorch, this can be implemented as:

```
def checkpointed_layer(layer, input):
    return torch.utils.checkpoint.checkpoint(layer, input)
```

When memory constraints force the use of small mini-batch sizes, training can become unstable due to high variance in gradient estimates. Gradient accumulation allows the model to process several microbatches, summing their gradients before performing an optimization update. This approach effectively simulates a larger batch size without exceeding memory limits:

35

```
optimizer.zero_grad()
for microbatch in batch_split(input_batch, microbatch_size):
    loss = model(microbatch).loss
    loss.backward()
optimizer.step()
```

Integrating the Solutions into a Training Pipeline

A robust training pipeline for LLMs integrates all these techniques. The optimizer (AdamW) manages the parameter updates adaptively, while the learning rate schedule ensures stability from the beginning of training to convergence. Memory efficiency methods like gradient checkpointing and accumulation make it feasible to train models that would otherwise exceed hardware limitations.

A simplified training loop might look like this:

```
for step in range(total_steps):
    optimizer.zero_grad() # Reset gradients at the beginning of each step
    for microbatch in microbatches(batch):
        # Use mixed precision to reduce memory usage and speed up computation
        with torch.autocast("cuda"):
            loss = model(microbatch).loss
        # Scale loss for numerical stability; accumulate gradients across
            microbatches
        scaler.scale(loss).backward()
    # Update model parameters using AdamW
    scaler.step(optimizer)
    # Update learning rate according to the warmup and cosine decay schedule
    scheduler.step()
    scaler.update()
```

The optimization problem in LLM training is multifaceted:

- **High Dimensionality and Noisy Gradients:** Adaptive optimizers like AdamW are used to scale learning rates per parameter and decouple weight decay, stabilizing training in complex loss landscapes.

- **Learning Rate Scheduling:** A dynamic schedule that starts with a warmup phase and transitions to cosine decay helps manage the size of updates, allowing for aggressive learning early on and fine-tuning as training converges.

- **Memory Constraints:** Techniques such as gradient checkpointing and gradient accumulation enable the training of very large models by reducing memory requirements without sacrificing the effective batch size.

Together, these strategies form a comprehensive optimization framework that ensures efficient, stable, and scalable training of large language models. By addressing the challenges head-on, this integrated approach allows practitioners to push the boundaries of model size and performance, even on hardware with limited resources.

2.5 Basic Evaluation Metrics

Evaluating large language models (LLMs) is a multi-dimensional challenge because different metrics capture different aspects of model performance. A robust evaluation framework not only helps in tracking improvements during pre-training and fine-tuning but also aids in diagnosing strengths and weaknesses of the model. In this section, we explain the key evaluation metrics, the underlying problems they address, and how they provide complementary insights into a model's performance.

The metrics discussed here fall into three broad categories:

1. **Fluency and Predictive Accuracy:** Measured by **perplexity**, this metric assesses how well the model predicts the next token given its context.

2. **Functional Correctness in Structured Tasks:** Measured by **pass@k** in code generation tasks, it evaluates whether the model can generate a correct solution among multiple attempts.

3. **Task-Specific Competence:** Measured by standardized reasoning, math, and general knowledge benchmarks, these tests probe the models ability to perform multi-step reasoning and recall factual information.

Below, we discuss each metric in detail, explain why it is used, and point out its limitations.

Perplexity: Measuring Fluency and Predictive Accuracy

The Problem: Capturing Statistical Fit of Language

During pre-training, a language model learns to predict the next token given the preceding context. However, a key challenge is determining how well the model has internalized the structure of the language. Perplexity serves

37

as a proxy for this predictive ability. It quantifies the model's uncertainty by measuring the average likelihood that the model assigns to each token in a test set.

Definition and Interpretation

Perplexity is defined as:

$$\text{Perplexity} = \exp\left(-\frac{1}{N}\sum_{t=1}^{N}\log p(x_t \mid x_1, x_2, \ldots, x_{t-1})\right),$$

where N is the total number of tokens. A lower perplexity indicates that the model is more confident about its predictions. For example, a perplexity of 10 implies that, on average, the models predictions are as uncertain as if it were choosing uniformly among 10 options.

Why It Matters and Its Limitations

Perplexity is useful because it directly reflects the fluency and statistical accuracy of the language model. However, it has its limitations:

- **Surface-Level Evaluation:** Perplexity primarily measures the models ability to capture local language structure but does not evaluate deeper reasoning or factual correctness.

- **Dependency on Tokenization:** Changes in tokenization schemes can affect perplexity, making cross-model comparisons challenging unless the tokenization is consistent.

A typical perplexity curve (see Figure 2.6) shows how perplexity decreases as training progresses, indicating improved predictive performance.

38

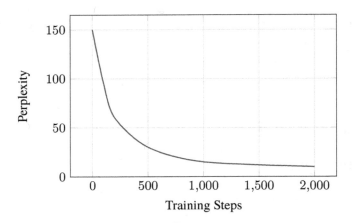

Figure 2.6: Typical perplexity curve during pre-training. A decrease in perplexity indicates that the model is better at predicting the next token.

Pass@k: Assessing Functional Correctness in Code Generation

When generating code, minor syntactic or logical errors can render a solution completely unusable. Unlike natural language, code requires exactness, and a single mistake can cause failure. To address this, pass@k is used to evaluate how often a model can generate a correct solution among multiple attempts.

For a set of programming problems, the model generates k independent solutions per problem. The pass@k metric is defined as:

$$\text{pass@k} = \frac{\text{Number of problems solved correctly by at least one solution}}{\text{Total number of problems}}.$$

For instance, if a model is evaluated on 100 problems and produces 5 candidate solutions per problem, and if at least one correct solution is generated for 72 problems, then:

$$\text{pass@5} = \frac{72}{100} = 0.72.$$

Why It Matters and Its Limitations

Pass@k is particularly important in contexts like competitive programming or code completion, where functional correctness is binary. However, it has its

39

own set of challenges:

- **Multiple Correct Approaches:** There can be multiple valid solutions to a coding problem. Pass@k must be interpreted with an understanding that it only measures the rate of obtaining at least one correct solution.

- **Dependency on k:** The value of k can significantly affect the metric. A larger k typically leads to a higher pass rate, but may also incur greater computational costs during evaluation.

Task-Specific Benchmarks: Evaluating Reasoning, Mathematics, and General Knowledge

While perplexity and pass@k focus on fluency and correctness in specific domains, they do not capture a models ability to reason, solve complex problems, or recall factual information. To address this, task-specific benchmarks are employed.

Reasoning Benchmarks:

- **GSM8K:** A dataset of grade-school math word problems that requires multi-step reasoning.

- **MATH:** A set of competition-level math problems that test deeper mathematical reasoning.

- **AQuA:** A collection of analytical questions that demand logical inference and reasoning.

For example, a GSM8K problem might ask: *John has 12 apples. He gives 4 to his friend and buys 7 more. How many apples does he have now?* A reasoning-capable model should decompose this into steps (start with 12, subtract 4, add 7) to arrive at the correct answer, 15.

General Knowledge Benchmarks:

- **TriviaQA:** A dataset consisting of open-domain questions covering a wide range of topics.

- **NaturalQuestions:** Real-world questions sourced from actual user queries.

- **OpenBookQA:** A benchmark that tests scientific knowledge and the ability to apply it.

For instance, a TriviaQA question may be: *Who painted the ceiling of the Sistine Chapel?* A factually knowledgeable model should answer:

Michelangelo.

Why Multiple Benchmarks are Necessary

No single metric can capture all facets of an LLMs performance. Perplexity measures how well a model predicts language at a surface level, while pass@k evaluates its ability to produce functionally correct outputs in constrained tasks like code generation. Meanwhile, reasoning and general knowledge benchmarks assess deeper cognitive abilities, such as multi-step inference, problem solving, and factual recall.

Aggregating results across these benchmarks provides a more comprehensive picture of a models strengths and weaknesses. For example, a table summarizing performance might look like:

Benchmark	Score
GSM8K (Math)	87%
TriviaQA (General Knowledge)	78%
MATH (Competition Math)	62%

Table 2.4: Example performance across reasoning and general knowledge benchmarks

Evaluation in LLM development is not about finding a single best model; rather, it is about understanding the multifaceted performance of the model across different dimensions:

- **Perplexity** provides insight into how well the model has learned the statistical properties of language.

- **Pass@k** demonstrates the models capability to generate correct outputs in highly structured domains like code.

- **Task-specific benchmarks** reveal the models ability to reason, solve complex problems, and recall factual information.

A comprehensive evaluation framework uses all these metrics in tandem to guide model improvements and ensure that enhancements in one area (e.g., fluency) do not come at the expense of others (e.g., reasoning ability).

Robust evaluation metrics are indispensable for developing and refining large language models. While perplexity, pass@k, and specialized benchmarks each have their limitations, together they form a balanced toolkit that informs both model selection and future research directions. By understanding the nuances of these metrics, practitioners can better diagnose performance issues, track progress over time, and ultimately build models that are not only fluent and accurate but also capable of deep reasoning and knowledge recall.

Chapter 3

Techniques and Strategies Shaping DeepSeek Models

This chapter examines the theoretical foundations and distinctive design strategies that shape DeepSeeks large language models, particularly DeepSeek-R1. It covers how DeepSeek applies Mixture-of-Experts (MoE) for scalable capacity, adapts advanced techniques for long-context processing, and employs reinforcement learning to enhance reasoning ability. By combining these techniques with explicit modeling of structured reasoning processes, DeepSeek establishes a framework that prioritizes both computational efficiency and advanced cognitive capabilities.

3.1 Mixture-of-Experts (MoE) Architecture

The Mixture-of-Experts (MoE) architecture has emerged as a transformative design in deep learning, especially for scaling large language models (LLMs). By leveraging conditional computation, MoE allows models to dramatically increase their parameter count without incurring a proportional increase in computational cost at inference time. In this section, we provide a comprehensive overview of MoEits historical roots, theoretical foundations, and practical implementationwhile detailing how DeepSeek specifically harnesses this architecture to achieve state-of-the-art performance.

Historical Background and Motivation

The idea of employing multiple specialized experts in a model dates back to the 1990s, where ensemble learning techniques were widely explored. Early Mixture-of-Experts models combined several simple classifiers, each responsible for a specific region of the input space, and a gating mechanism to decide which expert to use for a given input. Although these early approaches demonstrated the benefits of model specialization, they were limited by computational resources and lacked the scalability required for modern applications.

With the advent of deep learning, researchers revisited the MoE paradigm and adapted it to work within neural network frameworks. The modern MoE architecture integrates into transformer models by replacing conventional feedforward networks with a bank of experts. This conditional computation approach enables only a subset of the experts to be activated for each input token. In effect, while the total number of parameters can be extremely large (often in the billions or trillions), the computational cost for each forward pass remains modest because only a small fraction of these parameters are used at a time.

Conceptual Foundations of Mixture-of-Experts

At its core, the MoE architecture is based on the principle of **conditional computation**. In traditional dense neural networks, every layer processes all input tokens using the full set of parameters. By contrast, an MoE layer is designed such that only a small, dynamically determined subset of its parametersorganized as expertsis activated for a given input.

Experts and the Gating Network: An MoE layer comprises multiple independent sub-networks, referred to as **experts**. Suppose there are E experts in the layer. Each expert is typically a simple feedforward network (FFN) that can process an input vector. When an input token x is fed into an MoE layer, a learned **gating network** computes a set of scores or probabilities that determine which experts will be activated. In most modern implementations, only k out of the E experts are chosen to process the inputthis is known as **top-k gating**. For example, if $k = 2$, then for each token only the two most relevant experts (as determined by the gating network) are used.

Why Sparse Activation Matters: The use of sparse activation through top-k gating means that even though the overall model may have billions of parameters, the computation performed on any given token is only a fraction of that.

This sparsity is the key to scaling up model capacity without incurring prohibitive inference costs. By enabling a model to selectively activate only the most relevant experts, MoE achieves a balance between capacity (i.e., a vast number of parameters) and efficiency.

Mathematical Formulation of MoE

To understand MoE from a mathematical perspective, consider a standard feed-forward network (FFN) in a transformer block:

$$\text{FFN}(x) = \sigma(xW_1 + b_1)W_2 + b_2,$$

where x is the input representation, W_1 and W_2 are weight matrices, b_1 and b_2 are biases, and σ is a non-linear activation function such as ReLU.

In an MoE layer, this FFN is replaced by a collection of experts. Let $\text{Expert}_i(x)$ denote the output of the i-th expert when processing the input x. A gating network produces a set of weights $g_i(x)$, where typically $g_i(x) \geq 0$ and $\sum_{i=1}^{E} g_i(x) = 1$. The output of the MoE layer is then given by:

$$y = \sum_{i=1}^{E} g_i(x) \cdot \text{Expert}_i(x).$$

In practice, however, we use top-k gating. This means that the gating network is constrained so that only the k experts with the highest scores have non-zero weights. For example, if $k = 2$, then

$$y = g_{i_1}(x) \cdot \text{Expert}_{i_1}(x) + g_{i_2}(x) \cdot \text{Expert}_{i_2}(x),$$

where i_1 and i_2 are the indices of the two experts with the highest gating scores for input x. This formulation reduces the computational burden, since only two experts' parameters are involved in computing y.

Gating Networks: Detailed Operation and Challenges

The gating network is central to the MoE architecture. It takes an input token representation and produces a probability distribution over the E experts. A typical implementation uses a linear transformation followed by a softmax:

$$g(x) = \text{softmax}(xW_g + b_g),$$

where W_g and b_g are the weight matrix and bias for the gating network. The softmax ensures that the outputs are non-negative and sum to one. To implement top-k gating, one common approach is to compute the full softmax and then set all but the top k entries to zero, renormalizing if necessary.

However, designing an effective gating network is challenging:

- **Training Instability:** Learning to correctly route tokens to the appropriate experts is a non-trivial optimization problem. If the gating network does not learn effectively, some experts might be overused while others are rarely activated.

- **Load Imbalance:** Without proper incentives, the model may converge to a state where a few experts handle most of the computation, while many remain underutilized. This imbalance not only wastes capacity but also leads to inefficient training.

- **Cold Start Issues:** Experts that are rarely chosen during early training might not receive enough updates, causing them to lag behind in performance. This "cold start" problem can hinder overall model convergence.

To mitigate load imbalance, researchers add an auxiliary loss term to encourage the gating network to distribute tokens more evenly across experts:

$$\mathcal{L}_{\text{balance}} = \lambda \cdot \text{KL}\left(p_{\text{observed}} \parallel p_{\text{uniform}}\right),$$

where p_{observed} is the distribution of tokens across experts and p_{uniform} is a uniform distribution. The hyperparameter λ controls the strength of this balancing term.

Architectural Placement of MoE in Transformers

In standard transformer architectures, each block consists of a multi-head self-attention layer followed by a feedforward network (FFN), with layer normalization and residual connections applied throughout:

$$h = \text{LayerNorm}(x + \text{MultiHeadAttention}(x)),$$

$$y = \text{LayerNorm}(h + \text{FFN}(h)).$$

In MoE transformers, the feedforward network is replaced by an MoE layer:

$$y = \text{LayerNorm}(h + \text{MoE}(h)).$$

This modular integration allows the model to retain the powerful self-attention mechanism for capturing token-to-token dependencies, while the MoE layer provides a scalable and efficient means of increasing model capacity. The MoE layer, through its conditional computation, offers the dual benefit of high capacity and reduced inference cost.

Detailed Illustrative Diagram

To visualize the MoE mechanism more comprehensively, consider the following diagram that outlines the flow of a token through an MoE layer with top-k gating:

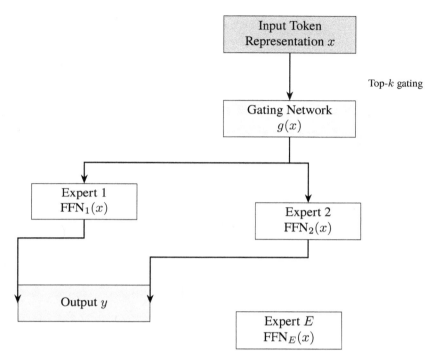

Figure 3.1: Illustrative diagram of an MoE layer. The input token representation is processed by a gating network, which selects the top-k experts (here, Expert 1 and Expert 2) to compute the output as a weighted sum.

In this diagram, the gating network computes the routing weights $g(x)$, and only the experts with the highest weights (e.g., Expert 1 and Expert 2) are activated. Their outputs are then combined to produce the final output, ensuring that only a small subset of the models parameters is used for each token.

Comparison to Dense Transformers

It is instructive to compare MoE transformers with conventional dense transformers. The table below summarizes key differences:

Aspect	Dense Transformer	MoE Transformer
Active Parameters per Token	Entire FFN	Only top-k experts
Total Model Capacity	Limited by GPU memory	Can be extremely large
Inference Cost	Fixed, high	Proportional to k (sparse)
Specialization	Homogeneous processing	Experts specialize in different patterns
Load Balancing	Not an issue	Requires auxiliary loss to balance expert usage

Table 3.1: Comparison between Dense and Mixture-of-Experts Transformers

This comparison highlights that while dense transformers use the entire network for every token, MoE transformers dynamically select a small subset of experts, allowing for enormous model capacity with only a fraction of the computational cost per token.

Trade-offs and Challenges in MoE Systems

Despite the benefits, MoE architectures come with inherent trade-offs and challenges:

Training Complexity: The gating network must learn to route tokens correctly, which adds an extra layer of complexity to the optimization process. Misrouted tokens can lead to suboptimal learning or even training instability.

Load Imbalance: Without careful regularization, the gating network might overuse certain experts while neglecting others. This imbalance can lead to inefficient use of model capacity. DeepSeek addresses this by introducing an auxiliary balancing loss that encourages a more uniform distribution of tokens across experts.

Communication Overhead: In distributed training setups, MoE layers can incur additional communication costs because expert activations may reside on different GPUs. Efficient communication strategies, such as optimized all-to-all operations, are critical to mitigate this overhead.

Cold Start for Experts: Experts that are rarely activated may not receive sufficient gradient updates, potentially leading to dead experts that contribute little to the overall performance. Special initialization strategies and adaptive regularization can help alleviate this problem.

How DeepSeek Implements MoE

DeepSeek models, such as DeepSeek-V3 and DeepSeek-R1, leverage the MoE architecture to scale up model capacity efficiently. Here are some specifics of DeepSeeks implementation:

1. Sparse Activation with Top-k Gating: DeepSeek uses top-k gating, where typically $k = 2$, meaning that for each token only the two most relevant experts are activated. This ensures that even though the total model capacity might be in the hundreds of billions of parameters, only a fraction (e.g., 37B active parameters) is used per token, significantly reducing computational cost.

2. Load Balancing Strategies: DeepSeek employs an auxiliary loss term designed to balance the load across experts. By penalizing deviations from a uniform distribution, the model ensures that no single expert is overburdened while others are underutilized. This balancing is critical for both training efficiency and achieving robust performance across various tasks.

3. Integration within the Transformer Block: In DeepSeeks architecture, the MoE layer replaces the conventional feedforward network (FFN) in the transformer block. The overall structure remains:

$$h = \text{LayerNorm}(x + \text{MultiHeadAttention}(x)),$$

$$y = \text{LayerNorm}(h + \text{MoE}(h)),$$

where $\text{MoE}(h)$ incorporates the expert networks and the gating mechanism. This design ensures that the benefits of self-attention are preserved while the computational efficiency of the feedforward pass is enhanced through sparse expert activation.

4. Scalability and Efficiency: By using the MoE architecture, DeepSeek models achieve massive scalability. For instance, DeepSeek-V3 boasts a total model size of 671 billion parameters, but thanks to sparse activation, only a fraction is used for each token. This design enables the model to harness the expressive power of a vast parameter set while keeping inference and training costs manageable.

Case Study: DeepSeek's MoE in Practice

Consider a scenario where DeepSeek-V3 is deployed for a complex language task requiring both general knowledge and domain-specific reasoning. In a dense transformer, every token would be processed by a massive, monolithic FFN, consuming substantial memory and computational resources. In contrast, DeepSeeks MoE implementation dynamically routes each token through only a couple of specialized experts, tailored to handle different aspects of the input. One expert might specialize in syntactic processing, while another might focus on semantic understanding or domain-specific terminology.

This conditional routing not only reduces the inference time but also allows each expert to develop specialized skills over the course of training. The gating network continuously learns which experts are best suited for different types of tokens. Over time, this leads to a model where experts become highly proficient in their respective niches, resulting in improved overall performance, particularly in challenging tasks that require nuanced understanding or reasoning.

Distributed Training Considerations

When training MoE models like those used in DeepSeek, additional complexities arise in distributed environments. Since experts are often spread across multiple GPUs or nodes, the model must handle:

- **Efficient Data Routing:** Ensuring that tokens are sent to the correct GPU where the corresponding expert resides.

- **Synchronized Updates:** Aggregating gradients from different GPUs to update the expert parameters correctly.

- **Communication Overhead:** Minimizing the time spent on data transfer between GPUs by using optimized all-to-all communication techniques.

DeepSeek addresses these challenges through careful co-design of algorithms and hardware-aware optimizations. Techniques such as overlapping communication with computation and using efficient network protocols ensure that the benefits of MoE are not offset by inter-device communication delays.

While the MoE architecture offers a powerful framework for scaling language models, several open research challenges remain:

- **Dynamic Expert Specialization:** Further work is needed to understand and improve how experts develop specialized knowledge over time and how to encourage diverse yet complementary expertise.

- **Adaptive Routing Mechanisms:** Developing more sophisticated gating networks that can adaptively adjust the number of experts activated based on input complexity or uncertainty.

- **Balancing Trade-offs:** Research on better load balancing methods that minimize communication overhead and training instability, especially in large-scale distributed settings.

- **Robustness and Generalization:** Investigating how MoE architectures perform on out-of-distribution tasks and ensuring that the specialization of experts does not lead to overfitting on narrow domains.

DeepSeek has put lots of effort exploring these avenues, aiming to further refine its MoE implementations and push the boundaries of what large-scale language models can achieve.

The Mixture-of-Experts architecture represents one of the most promising directions for scaling large language models efficiently. By allowing only a small, carefully chosen subset of experts to be active for each token, MoE enables the construction of models with enormous capacity without incurring prohibitive computational costs. The combination of conditional computation, expert specialization, and efficient load balancing underpins the success of MoE-based systems like DeepSeek-V3 and DeepSeek-R1. In summary, MoE offers:

- **Massive Model Capacity:** Enabling billions of parameters while maintaining efficient inference through sparse activation.

- **Expert Specialization:** Allowing different experts to learn and handle distinct aspects of the input data.

- **Cost-Effective Training:** Reducing computational and memory requirements via conditional computation and optimized routing.

By understanding both the theoretical foundations and the practical challenges, readers gain insight into why MoE has become a cornerstone for modern LLMs and how innovations like DeepSeeks implementation can drive further advances in the field. As the research community continues to address open challenges, the MoE paradigm is poised to play an increasingly critical role in developing models that are not only larger and more powerful but also more efficient and adaptable to diverse tasks.

3.2 Long-Context Support

Modern large language models (LLMs) are increasingly called upon to process lengthy documents, multi-file codebases, and extended dialogues. In many real-world applicationssuch as legal contract review, scientific paper analysis, and comprehensive code generationthe ability to handle long contexts is not just beneficial; it is essential. However, traditional transformer architectures were designed with relatively short input sequences in mind, typically ranging from 512 to 2048 tokens. Extending these models to support tens or hundreds of thousands of tokens introduces a host of theoretical and practical challenges.

The practical applications of LLMs often extend beyond the processing of short text snippets. Many tasks require the model to comprehend and reason over entire documents or collections of files. Consider the following examples:

- **Legal Analysis:** Legal documents and contracts can be tens of thousands of words long. The ability to capture long-range dependencies is critical to understand clauses, exceptions, and interdependencies that span the entire document.

- **Scientific Literature:** Research papers and technical reports often contain detailed arguments and derivations spread over many pages. Understanding the full context is crucial for tasks such as summarization and hypothesis generation.

- **Multi-file Codebases:** Software projects consist of many interdependent files. For tasks such as bug detection or code completion, the model must be aware of definitions and functions that could be separated by thousands of lines of code.

- **Long-Form Dialogue:** In conversational agents, maintaining context over long conversations improves coherence and personalization.

Short context lengths limit the models ability to capture these dependencies. For example, if a code generation model is trained only on 4K tokens, it might fail to recognize that a critical library import or class definition appears 5K tokens earlier, leading to errors in the generated code. Thus, supporting long contexts not only broadens the range of applications but also significantly enhances the models reasoning and generative capabilities.

Theoretical Challenges: Quadratic Complexity of Self-Attention

The primary architectural challenge in processing long sequences stems from the self-attention mechanism. In a standard transformer, the self-attention operation computes pairwise interactions between all tokens in a sequence. If the sequence length is n and the embedding dimension is d, the query Q and key K matrices have dimensions $(n \times d)$. The computation of the attention scores is performed as:

$$A = \frac{QK^T}{\sqrt{d}},$$

resulting in an $n \times n$ attention matrix. This leads to a computational and memory complexity of $O(n^2 d)$. For instance, with a sequence of 128K tokens, even with moderate embedding dimensions, the full attention matrix would contain over 16 billion entries. Such quadratic scaling quickly becomes infeasible on current hardware.

This quadratic cost is the central obstacle to long-context support. It not only increases computation time but also demands enormous memory bandwidth and storage. To mitigate these issues, researchers have developed alternative attention mechanisms that approximate full attention at a significantly reduced computational cost.

Advanced Positional Encoding: Rotary Positional Embeddings (RoPE)

Traditional transformers incorporate positional information by adding sinusoidal positional encodings to token embeddings. These fixed encodings work well for sequences that fall within the range seen during training, but they do not extrapolate effectively to much longer sequences. Rotary Positional Embeddings (RoPE) provide a solution by embedding positional information directly into the attention mechanism.

How RoPE Works: RoPE operates by rotating the query and key vectors according to their position in the sequence. Formally, for a given token at position i, the query vector q_i is transformed by a rotation matrix $R(i)$:

$$\tilde{q}_i = R(i)\, q_i,$$

and similarly for the key vectors:

$$\tilde{k}_i = R(i)\, k_i.$$

The rotation matrix $R(i)$ is designed such that the dot product between rotated vectors depends solely on the relative distance between their positions, i.e.,

$$\tilde{q}_i^T \tilde{k}_j = q_i^T R(i)^T R(j) k_j,$$

which depends on $j - i$. This approach inherently provides *translation invariance*: the attention score between two tokens is a function of their distance, not their absolute positions. This quality is crucial for generalizing to contexts much longer than those seen during training.

Benefits of RoPE:

- **Extrapolation:** RoPE allows the model to naturally generalize to longer sequences without retraining the positional encodings.

- **Improved Relative Positioning:** By directly incorporating relative positions into the attention computation, RoPE can capture dependencies that span long distances.

- **Seamless Integration:** RoPE is easily integrated into existing transformer architectures by replacing the traditional positional encoding scheme.

Memory-Efficient Attention Mechanisms

Even with advanced positional embeddings like RoPE, computing full self-attention over extremely long sequences is prohibitively expensive. To address this, several strategies have been developed to reduce the memory and computation requirements.

Chunked Attention

One approach is **chunked attention**, which divides the long sequence into smaller, overlapping windows (chunks) and computes attention only within each window. This method reduces the computational complexity from $O(n^2)$ to roughly $O(nw)$, where w is the window size. Although this may cause the model to miss some long-range dependencies between distant chunks, overlapping windows help mitigate this issue.

Sparse Attention

Another promising technique is **sparse attention**, which allows each token to attend only to a subset of other tokens. For example, a token may attend to its w nearest neighbors and a few global tokens that summarize the sequence. In some implementations, the complexity can be reduced to $O(n \log n)$ or even $O(n)$, depending on the sparsity pattern. Sparse attention balances the need to capture local details with the requirement to model long-range dependencies.

Sliding Window Attention

Sliding window attention is a specific instance of sparse attention. Here, each token's attention is restricted to a fixed-size window around it:

$$
A_{ij} = \begin{cases} \frac{q_i \cdot k_j}{\sqrt{d}}, & \text{if } |i - j| \leq w, \\ 0, & \text{otherwise.} \end{cases}
$$

This method preserves local structure efficiently but may need additional mechanisms (e.g., dilated windows or global tokens) to capture dependencies that lie outside the window.

Comparative Analysis of Attention Mechanisms

The following figure illustrates how the memory cost of different attention mechanisms scales with sequence length:

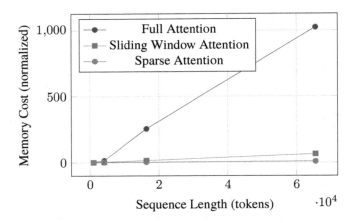

Figure 3.2: Memory cost growth for full, sliding window, and sparse attention mechanisms.

Training Strategies for Long-Context Models

Even with the theoretical improvements in attention mechanisms, models trained exclusively on short sequences tend to struggle when exposed to long contexts. This challenge is often described in terms of **positional drift** and **vanishing relevance**, where the model does not learn to assign sufficient importance to tokens that are far apart. To address this, two key training strategies are employed:

Curriculum Learning with Progressive Context Extension

One effective strategy is to gradually increase the sequence length during traininga method akin to curriculum learning. In early training stages, the model is trained on relatively short sequences. As training progresses, the context length is gradually extended until it reaches the target (e.g., 128K tokens). This gradual increase allows the model to adapt its parameters to handle longer sequences without being overwhelmed by the computational burden or noise from extremely long contexts.

57

Curated Long-Context Data

Another critical factor is the quality and relevance of the training data. For a model to handle long contexts, it must be exposed to long-form documents during training. Curated datasets for long-context training include:

- **Books and Academic Papers:** Texts with consistent narrative flow and complex interdependencies.

- **Legal and Contract Documents:** These texts require understanding of clauses and references spread over large sections.

- **Multi-File Code Repositories:** Codebases that require cross-file dependency resolution.

- **Extended Conversations:** Transcripts of meetings or dialogues that capture long-term context.

Including such data in the training corpus ensures that the model learns to capture dependencies over long spans and does not solely focus on short-range correlations.

DeepSeek s Long-Context Strategy

DeepSeek implements a multi-pronged strategy to achieve support for 128K-token contexts. This strategy integrates theoretical advancements, training methodologies, and data curation practices:

1. Advanced Positional Encoding: DeepSeek replaces traditional sinusoidal encodings with Rotary Positional Embeddings (RoPE). By rotating the query and key vectors based on token positions, RoPE encodes relative positional information effectively. This method ensures that the models performance does not deteriorate when the sequence length exceeds the training range. The translation invariance provided by RoPE means that the attention between two tokens depends only on their relative distance, which is vital for maintaining coherence in long sequences.

2. Efficient Attention Mechanisms: To manage the quadratic complexity of full self-attention, DeepSeek employs a combination of sparse and sliding window attention. In practice, the model uses a sparse attention mechanism that reduces the number of computed attention weights, while also incorporating a sliding window approach to capture local context efficiently. These methods reduce memory usage and computational cost, making it feasible to handle sequences as long as 128K tokens.

3. Curriculum Learning and Data Curation: DeepSeek trains its long-context models using a curriculum learning approach. Early training stages focus on shorter sequences to establish a strong base model. As training proceeds, the sequence length is gradually increased until the model is exposed to the full 128K-token context. Furthermore, DeepSeek curates a specialized dataset containing long-form documents, multi-file projects, and extended dialogues. This curated data ensures that the model learns to handle long-range dependencies effectively.

4. Hybrid Approaches for Extreme Contexts: For some applications, even 128K tokens may not suffice. While DeepSeeks core strategy is to extend the context within the model, hybrid approaches that combine long-context transformers with external memory (such as retrieval-augmented generation systems) are also explored. These systems can access external data repositories to supplement the models internal context, although such methods are beyond the scope of DeepSeeks primary design.

Evaluation and Trade-Offs

Supporting long contexts introduces trade-offs that must be carefully balanced:

- **Increased Training Cost:** Longer sequences increase computational cost per sample and may slow down training. DeepSeek mitigates this through optimized attention mechanisms and mixed-precision training.

- **Positional Drift:** Models trained on short contexts may not extrapolate well to longer ones. The use of RoPE and curriculum learning helps minimize positional drift, but careful monitoring during training is necessary.

- **Local vs. Global Dependencies:** While sliding window attention efficiently captures local context, it may miss global dependencies. Sparse attention patterns, often combined with global tokens, are designed to address this issue, though finding the right balance remains an active area of research.

- **Memory and Compute Constraints:** Even with efficient approximations, processing 128K-token sequences demands significant memory.
DeepSeeks approach integrates both architectural improvements and
hardware-aware optimizations to make such large contexts tractable.

The benefits of these trade-offs are evident in application. For example, in
tasks such as contract analysis or multi-file code understanding, a model that
supports long contexts can maintain coherence across document sections that
are separated by thousands of tokens. Evaluation on long-context benchmarks
shows that models like DeepSeek, which employ these strategies, outperform
counterparts that are limited to shorter contexts.

Visualizing the Impact of Long Contexts

To illustrate the effect of long-context support, consider the following
schematic diagram comparing the memory cost growth for different attention
mechanisms as sequence length increases:

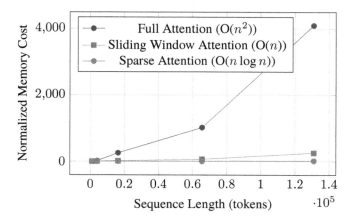

Figure 3.3: Memory cost scaling for different attention mechanisms. Note the
dramatic increase in cost for full attention, versus the more modest growth for
sliding window and sparse attention.

This diagram clearly shows that while full attention scales quadratically with
sequence length, sparse and sliding window techniques significantly reduce

the memory footprint, enabling practical long-context processing.

DeepSeek s Specific Implementation and Innovations

DeepSeek leverages a combination of the techniques discussed above to support a 128K-token context. Some of the specific innovations include:

Enhanced Rotary Positional Embeddings: DeepSeek refines the RoPE method to better accommodate extremely long sequences. This includes calibrating the rotation parameters to ensure that the relative positional information remains accurate over longer distances, thereby preventing positional drift.

Hybrid Attention Mechanisms: DeepSeek s architecture incorporates both sparse attention and sliding window strategies. This hybrid approach enables the model to capture both local and long-range dependencies efficiently. The model dynamically selects the appropriate attention mechanism based on the input structure, ensuring that critical long-range connections are not lost while minimizing unnecessary computations.

Curriculum and Data Augmentation: During training, DeepSeek adopts a curriculum learning approach. Initially, the model is trained on short sequences (e.g., 4K tokens) to build a strong foundational understanding of language. As training progresses, the context length is gradually increased to the target 128K tokens. In parallel, the training data is augmented with a curated corpus of long-context documents, including entire books, academic articles, legal documents, and multi-file code repositories. This ensures that the model learns to process extended contexts effectively.

Distributed Training Optimizations: Handling long sequences requires careful orchestration across multiple GPUs. DeepSeek optimizes inter-device communication by overlapping computation and communication. Efficient all-to-all communication kernels and optimized data routing protocols are employed so that the benefits of long-context support are not negated by communication overhead.

Evaluation on Long-Context Tasks: DeepSeek s long-context capabilities are rigorously evaluated on benchmarks designed for extended sequences. Tasks such as multi-file code generation, long-form summarization, and comprehensive document analysis serve as testbeds. Early results indicate that the ability to maintain context over 128K tokens leads to significant improvements

61

in tasks that require understanding and reasoning over long documents.

Trade-Offs and Limitations

While the advancements in long-context support are promising, they come with trade-offs:

- **Computational Overhead:** Even with sparse attention, processing 128K tokens is computationally intensive. This requires significant hardware resources and may limit the models applicability in low-resource environments.

- **Model Complexity:** The combination of multiple attention mechanisms, advanced positional encodings, and curriculum learning increases the overall complexity of the model architecture, which can make debugging and further development more challenging.

- **Task-Specific Benefits:** Not all tasks benefit equally from extended context. For applications where relevant information is contained within a shorter span, the additional complexity may not yield proportional gains.

- **Evaluation Challenges:** Standard benchmarks for long-context reasoning are still under development. Without well-established evaluation protocols, it can be difficult to quantify the exact benefits of extended context support.

Despite these limitations, the benefits in domains that require long-term dependency modeling are substantial. The careful balance of efficiency, scalability, and model performance makes these trade-offs acceptable for many high-impact applications.

Long-context support represents one of the most significant advancements in the evolution of large language models. By addressing the quadratic complexity of traditional self-attention, utilizing advanced techniques like Rotary Positional Embeddings and sparse attention, and employing curriculum learning alongside carefully curated long-context data, models like DeepSeek are able to process up to 128K tokens in a single forward pass. This breakthrough opens up new possibilities for applications that require a comprehensive understanding of lengthy documents, extensive codebases, and multi-step reasoning processes.

Through this integrated approach, DeepSeek not only pushes the boundaries of context length in language modeling but also lays the groundwork for more advanced reasoning and understanding capabilities in real-world applications. As research in this area continues to evolve, further refinements in attention efficiency, positional encoding, and training strategies will be critical to fully harness the potential of long-context models.

3.3 Reinforcement Learning for Reasoning

Large language models (LLMs) have demonstrated remarkable capabilities in generating fluent text and recalling factual information through extensive pre-training. However, when it comes to tasks that require multi-step logical reasoning, such as solving complex math problems, constructing logical proofs, or generating structured code, the traditional objectives of next-token prediction and even supervised fine-tuning fall short. This section explains the limitations of pre-training and supervised learning for reasoning, introduces the fundamentals of reinforcement learning (RL) for reasoning, and describes DeepSeeks specific approachincluding its Group Relative Policy Optimization (GRPO) and reward modeling techniquesto enhance reasoning quality in its models.

Limitations of Pre-training and Supervised Fine-Tuning

Pre-training generally involves training a model to predict the next token given a prior context. Although this method effectively captures grammar, syntax, and factual correlations, it does not necessarily encourage the model to develop a coherent, step-by-step reasoning process. For example, consider the following simple math problem:

If a square has a side length of 5, what is its area?

A model trained solely by next-token prediction might simply memorize the fact that the area is 25, without learning to derive the answer using the underlying principles:

1. Recall the formula: $A = s^2$.

2. Substitute $s = 5$.

3. Compute $A = 25$.

Similarly, even supervised fine-tuning (SFT) where the model is trained on curated examples typically optimizes for token-level overlap with a target answer. While SFT can help the model learn the format of explanations, it does not explicitly incentivize the intermediate logical steps that constitute true reasoning. In both cases, the training objective does not reward the process; it rewards only the final outcome.

The Rationale for Reinforcement Learning in Reasoning

To address this gap, reinforcement learning (RL) is employed to directly optimize the models reasoning process. In RL, the model (or agent) interacts with an environment and receives a reward based on the quality of its outputs. The key idea is to shape the models behavior by rewarding not just the correct final answer but also the intermediate steps that lead to that answer.

Core RL Concepts

In the RL framework, the model follows a policy π_θ (parameterized by θ) that generates a sequence of tokens $x = (x_1, x_2, \ldots, x_T)$. The training objective is to maximize the expected reward:

$$\max_\theta \mathbb{E}_{x \sim \pi_\theta}[r(x)],$$

where $r(x)$ is a reward function that evaluates the quality of the generated reasoning process. Unlike pre-training, where the objective is simply to predict the next token, the RL objective considers the overall quality of the reasoningrewarding clarity, logical consistency, and correctness.

Benefits of RL for Reasoning

The use of RL for reasoning offers several important advantages:

- **Process-Oriented Learning:** RL enables the model to be rewarded for generating a detailed chain-of-thought (CoT) rather than only for arriving at the correct final answer.

- **Exploration of Multiple Strategies:** By sampling various reasoning paths and comparing their rewards, the model can explore and discover more effective problem-solving strategies.

- **Alignment with Human Judgment:** When the reward function is designed to reflect human preferencessuch as clarity, logical progression, and completenessthe models reasoning becomes more interpretable and aligned with human expectations.

Group Relative Policy Optimization (GRPO)

A critical challenge in applying RL to reasoning is the high variance and noise in the reward signal, which can lead to instability during training. DeepSeek addresses this challenge by using a specialized variant of Proximal Policy Optimization (PPO) called Group Relative Policy Optimization (GRPO).

Understanding GRPO

Standard PPO updates the policy based on the absolute reward of each sampled output. However, in the context of reasoning, it is more beneficial to compare the quality of different reasoning paths generated for the same task. GRPO does exactly that by evaluating candidate completions within a group, assigning higher rewards to those that outperform others.

The GRPO objective is given by:

$$L_{\text{GRPO}} = \mathbb{E}\left[\log \pi_\theta(x \mid x_0) \cdot \frac{e^{r(x)}}{\sum_{x' \in G} e^{r(x')}}\right],$$

where:

- x_0 is the initial prompt.

- G is the group of candidate completions generated for the same prompt.

- $r(x)$ is the reward assigned to a particular reasoning path.

This formulation encourages the model to favor reasoning paths that are relatively superior to other candidates for the same task. By focusing on relative improvements, GRPO helps reduce the variance typically seen in standard RL training, leading to more stable convergence.

Advantages of Relative Comparison

The relative reward signal in GRPO aligns more closely with human evaluation, where the quality of reasoning is often judged in comparison to alternative approaches. This method not only promotes correct answers but also emphasizes the quality of the reasoning process, including clarity, logical flow, and adherence to a step-by-step format.

Reward Modeling for Reasoning Quality

For reinforcement learning to effectively improve reasoning, the reward model must capture multiple dimensions of what constitutes good reasoning. DeepSeeks reward model evaluates completions based on several key factors:

- **Correctness:** The final answer must be accurate.

- **Clarity:** The reasoning process should be clearly articulated, with each step logically following from the previous one.

- **Completeness and Format:** The explanation should be structured in a way that mirrors a human-like chain-of-thought, including intermediate steps and explanations.

The combined reward function is expressed as:

$$r(x) = \lambda_1 \, r_{\text{correct}}(x) + \lambda_2 \, r_{\text{clarity}}(x) + \lambda_3 \, r_{\text{format}}(x),$$

where λ_1, λ_2, and λ_3 are coefficients that balance the contribution of each component. This multi-objective reward ensures that the model does not merely focus on producing the correct final answer, but also learns to articulate the reasoning process in a coherent and transparent manner.

Training the Reward Model

The reward model is itself trained using supervised learning. A dataset of reasoning completions is collected and scored by human annotators or automated tools. For math problems, symbolic solvers can be used to verify correctness, while human raters assess clarity and logical structure. This reward model is then used during the RL phase to assign reward values to the candidate reasoning paths generated by the model.

66

The Reinforcement Learning Pipeline for Reasoning

DeepSeek s RL pipeline for improving reasoning can be broken down into several key stages:

Stage 1: Base Model Pre-training

Initially, the base model is pre-trained on massive text corpora using next-token prediction. This stage imparts general language fluency and factual knowledge, but it does not optimize for the explicit reasoning process.

Stage 2: Reward Model Training

Next, a reward model is trained on a dataset of reasoning completions. This dataset includes examples of high-quality chain-of-thought explanations, annotated for correctness, clarity, and format. The reward model learns to predict a reward score $r(x)$ for any given reasoning process.

Stage 3: Reinforcement Learning via GRPO

Once the reward model is ready, the base model is fine-tuned using reinforcement learning. For each prompt x_0, the model generates a group G of candidate completions. Using the GRPO objective, the model is updated based on the relative quality of these completions. This encourages the model to explore various reasoning paths and adopt those that yield higher overall rewards.

Stage 4: Rejection Sampling and Fine-Tuning

After the RL phase, the model generates multiple reasoning completions for each prompt. Rejection sampling is then applied to select the best candidate i.e., the one with the highest reward score:

$$x^* = \arg \max_{x \in \{x_1, \ldots, x_k\}} r(x).$$

This best completion is used for further fine-tuning, ensuring that only high-quality reasoning processes are reinforced in the final model.

Illustrative Diagram of the RL Pipeline

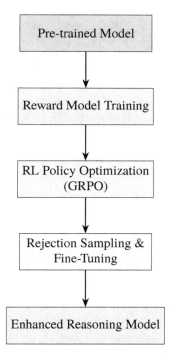

Figure 3.4: The reinforcement learning pipeline for enhancing reasoning in LLMs.

Example: Mathematical Reasoning

To illustrate the benefits of reinforcement learning for reasoning, consider a multi-step math problem:

If a rectangle has a length of 8 and a width of 3, what is its area?

A conventional pre-trained model might output the correct answer "24" without revealing its thought process. In contrast, with reinforcement learning, the model is encouraged to generate an explanation such as:

1. Recall the formula for the area of a rectangle: $A = \text{length} \times \text{width}$.

2. Substitute the given values: $A = 8 \times 3$.

3. Calculate the product: $A = 24$.

The reward model assigns a high score to this detailed chain-of-thought based on its correctness, clarity, and structured presentation. Through GRPO, the model learns that producing such detailed explanations consistently results in higher rewards compared to simply outputting the final answer.

Advantages and Impact of RL on Reasoning

The primary advantages of applying reinforcement learning to enhance reasoning are as follows:

- **Improved Process Transparency:** The model is encouraged to output intermediate reasoning steps, which improves interpretability and makes the decision-making process transparent. This is critical for applications where understanding the rationale behind an answer is as important as the answer itself.

- **Enhanced Generalization:** By exploring various reasoning paths during training, the model learns to tackle complex and novel problems more effectively. This exploration fosters robust generalization, particularly in tasks that require multi-step inference.

- **Alignment with Human Judgement:** The reward model, trained on human-annotated data, ensures that the model's reasoning aligns with human expectations for clarity, logical flow, and completeness. This alignment helps in building trust and usability in real-world applications.

- **Task-Specific Optimization:** Reinforcement learning allows the model to tailor its reasoning strategies to specific domains, such as mathematical problem-solving or code generation. By directly optimizing for reasoning quality, the model becomes more adept at handling domain-specific challenges.

Challenges and Trade-offs

Despite its many benefits, the reinforcement learning approach for reasoning introduces several challenges:

- **Training Instability:** RL training is inherently more unstable than supervised learning due to the high variance in reward signals. Techniques like GRPO help mitigate this issue by comparing candidate completions within a group, but careful tuning of learning rates and reward scaling is essential.

- **Designing the Reward Function:** Crafting a reward function that accurately captures all facets of good reasoning is complex. An overemphasis on one component (e.g., brevity) might lead the model to produce overly terse explanations, while a reward function that is too complex can hinder the training process. Balancing correctness, clarity, and format is a delicate task.

- **Computational Overhead:** Generating multiple candidate reasoning paths for each prompt and evaluating them with the reward model increases the computational burden. This added cost is a trade-off for the improved quality of reasoning and may require substantial computational resources.

- **Scalability and Efficiency:** As the complexity of the reasoning tasks increases, ensuring that the RL framework scales without sacrificing performance remains a significant challenge. Further research is needed to explore adaptive or hierarchical reinforcement learning strategies that can manage increasingly complex tasks.

- **Interpretability and Debugging:** Even though RL encourages more transparent reasoning processes, interpreting the internal decision-making process of the model remains difficult. Developing better visualization and debugging tools is crucial for understanding why the model prefers one reasoning path over another.

Integration with DeepSeeks Overall Strategy

DeepSeek s reinforcement learning framework for reasoning is designed to complement its broader training pipeline. Here are some key aspects of how

70

DeepSeek integrates RL into its system:

- **Sequential Training Phases:** DeepSeek first trains its base model using conventional pre-training on vast datasets to capture general language fluency and factual knowledge. The RL phase is then applied specifically to enhance reasoning capabilities, refining the models ability to generate detailed chains-of-thought.

- **Task-Focused Reward Modeling:** The reward model in DeepSeek is carefully designed to evaluate reasoning quality across multiple dimensions. By combining automated metrics (such as symbolic validation for math problems) with human-annotated feedback, DeepSeek ensures that the reward function aligns closely with the desired qualities in a reasoning process.

- **Iterative Refinement and Rejection Sampling:** DeepSeek uses an iterative approach in which the RL phase is followed by a rejection sampling step. In this step, multiple candidate reasoning paths are generated for each prompt, and the best oneaccording to the reward modelis selected for further fine-tuning. This iterative refinement ensures that only high-quality reasoning is reinforced.

- **Relative Comparison through GRPO:** By using Group Relative Policy Optimization (GRPO), DeepSeek encourages the model to evaluate and compare multiple reasoning paths for the same problem. This relative comparison helps the model learn to favor strategies that yield the highest quality output, leading to more robust reasoning performance.

Reinforcement learning for reasoning represents a significant advancement over traditional pre-training and supervised fine-tuning. By directly rewarding the process of multi-step reasoning, DeepSeeks RL framework addresses the shortcomings of conventional training methods, which often neglect the importance of a coherent chain-of-thought. The integration of specialized techniques such as GRPO, sophisticated reward modeling, and iterative refinement through rejection sampling enables the model not only to generate correct answers but also to explain its reasoning in a clear, logical, and interpretable manner.

While challenges such as training instability, computational overhead, and reward function design persist, the benefits of this approach are substantial. Enhanced reasoning capability leads to improved performance on complex tasks

71

such as multi-step mathematical problem solving, logical proofs, and detailed code generation. Moreover, by aligning the models internal processes with human judgment, DeepSeeks reinforcement learning strategy paves the way for more transparent and trustworthy AI systems.

In summary, reinforcement learning for reasoning transforms the models objective from merely predicting the next token to generating a coherent, step-by-step explanation that reflects true logical understanding. This shift is critical for applications where the quality of reasoning is as important as the final output. As research in this area continues to evolve, further innovations in reward modeling, RL algorithms, and hybrid training approaches will likely drive even greater improvements in the reasoning capabilities of large language models.

3.4 Chain-of-Thought Modeling

In many complex tasks, a correct final answer is only part of the solution; the process by which the answer is reached is equally critical. Humans solve problems by breaking them down into a series of logical, step-by-step reasoning processesa chain-of-thought (CoT). However, traditional training objectives for large language models (LLMs), such as next-token prediction or even supervised fine-tuning, generally optimize only for the final output without explicitly encouraging intermediate steps. Chain-of-thought modeling addresses this gap by training models to *show their work*, producing transparent and interpretable reasoning paths. In this section, we explain the motivation behind chain-of-thought modeling, the theoretical foundations underlying it, the training techniques used to enforce structured reasoning, and the specific methods implemented in DeepSeek. We also discuss the benefits, challenges, and future directions of this approach.

Motivation for Chain-of-Thought Modeling

Most conventional LLMs are trained to generate the most likely sequence of tokens, which works well for language fluency and factual recall. However, when faced with multi-step reasoning taskssuch as solving math problems, generating complex code, or analyzing legal documentsmerely producing a correct final answer is insufficient. Consider the example from last section:

If a rectangle has a length of 8 and a width of 3, what is its area?

A model that is not explicitly trained for reasoning might simply output "24" based on memorization. In contrast, human problem solvers typically articulate a series of steps:

1. Recall the formula: $A = \text{length} \times \text{width}$.

2. Substitute the values: $A = 8 \times 3$.

3. Compute the result: $A = 24$.

Chain-of-thought modeling aims to encourage models to generate such step-by-step explanations. This has several advantages:

- **Transparency:** A clear reasoning process allows users to verify and trust the model's conclusions.

- **Partial Credit:** Even if the final answer is slightly off, correct intermediate reasoning can be identified and rewarded.

- **Error Diagnosis:** Detailed reasoning helps in pinpointing where the model may have gone wrong, facilitating further improvements.

- **Generalization:** Models that learn to reason explicitly can generalize better to novel or more complex tasks.

Theoretical Foundations: Process vs. Outcome Supervision

Traditional training methods for LLMs are based on **outcome supervision**. In this approach, the model is trained to minimize a loss function that compares the generated output y_{pred} with the ground-truth output y_{true}:

$$\min_{\theta} \text{Loss}(y_{\text{pred}}, y_{\text{true}}).$$

This formulation does not enforce that the model produces intermediate reasoning stepsit only cares about the final result.

In chain-of-thought modeling, we introduce **process supervision**. Here, the goal is to train the model not only to produce the correct answer but also to

73

generate a sequence of reasoning steps $s = (s_1, s_2, \ldots, s_n)$ that lead to that answer. The training objective becomes:

$$\min_{\theta} \sum_{i=1}^{n} \text{Loss}(s_{\text{pred}}^i, s_{\text{true}}^i),$$

where s_{pred}^i is the models predicted output at step i, and s_{true}^i is the corresponding ground-truth step. This formulation explicitly encourages the model to show its work by decomposing a problem into logical intermediate steps.

Techniques for Chain-of-Thought Modeling

To enable chain-of-thought reasoning, several techniques are employed during training:

Explicit Process Markers

One effective method is to insert explicit process markers into the training data. These markers delineate each reasoning step and serve as cues for the model. For example, in a math problem, the training text might be annotated as follows:

```
<think> Step 1: Define the variables and recall the formula </think>
<think> Step 2: Substitute the given values into the formula </think>
<think> Step 3: Compute the result </think>
```

These markers act as a structural guide, teaching the model that a coherent explanation is composed of distinct, ordered steps. By providing explicit signals during training, the model learns to generate similar markers during inference.

Process Templates and Structured Formats

In addition to markers, predefined templates help standardize the reasoning process. For instance, a template for solving geometry problems might require the model to:

1. Restate the problem in its own words.

2. List all known variables.

74

3. Write down the relevant formulas.

4. Substitute values and perform computations.

5. Provide the final answer with an explanation.

Training on such structured data conditions the model to output answers in a consistent, interpretable format. This consistency not only improves clarity but also facilitates evaluation, as the reasoning process can be compared against human standards.

Reflection and Self-Verification

A further innovation in chain-of-thought modeling is the incorporation of self-reflection. After generating a reasoning process, the model is prompted to review its work and check for errors. For example:

```
Q: Solve for x in the equation x^2 - 5x + 6 = 0.
A:
<think> Step 1: Identify coefficients a=1, b=-5, c=6 </think>
<think> Step 2: Apply the quadratic formula: x = (5 (25-24))/2 </think>
<think> Step 3: Compute x = 3 and x = 2 </think>
Q: Now, review your steps and verify their correctness.
```

This self-verification loop encourages the model to check its reasoning for internal consistency. It mirrors human problem-solving practices and provides an additional layer of quality control during training.

Reinforcement Learning Integration

While explicit process markers and templates guide the model during supervised fine-tuning, reinforcement learning (RL) further refines the chain-of-thought. In RL, the model is treated as an agent that generates a sequence of reasoning steps and receives a reward based on the quality of its output. The reward function can be designed to consider multiple aspects:

$$r(x) = \lambda_1 \, r_{\text{correct}}(x) + \lambda_2 \, r_{\text{clarity}}(x) + \lambda_3 \, r_{\text{format}}(x).$$

Here, the reward model evaluates the generated chain-of-thought for correctness, clarity, and adherence to the expected structure. Techniques like Group

Relative Policy Optimization (GRPO) are used to compare different reasoning paths generated for the same problem, guiding the model toward the best-performing process. This relative evaluation is key in reducing variance in the reward signal and ensuring that the model learns to generate high-quality, coherent reasoning steps.

Application in DeepSeek

DeepSeek has integrated chain-of-thought modeling into its training pipeline to improve the reasoning capabilities of its models, such as DeepSeek-R1. The process involves several stages:

Data Preparation with Process Annotations

During the data curation phase, DeepSeek enriches its training data with explicit annotations. For example, a dataset for mathematical problem solving might include:

```
Q: What is the sum of angles in a triangle?
A:
<think> Step 1: Recall that the sum of angles in a triangle is given by a known
        theorem </think>
<think> Step 2: State the theorem: The sum is 180 degrees </think>
<think> Step 3: Conclude that the sum of the given triangle's angles is 180
        degrees </think>
```

Such annotated data teaches the model to produce multi-step, coherent reasoning rather than simply memorizing answers.

Template-Based Supervised Fine-Tuning

DeepSeek further refines its models by fine-tuning them on a structured dataset that follows predefined reasoning templates. For example, a template for code generation might include:

1. An explanation of the problem context.

2. A step-by-step breakdown of the algorithm or logic.

3. Detailed comments on how each part of the code solves the problem.

4. The final code snippet along with a summary of the solution.

This standardized format helps the model learn not only to generate the correct final output but also to articulate the process leading up to it.

Reinforcement Learning with GRPO and Self-Reflection

After supervised fine-tuning, DeepSeek applies reinforcement learning to further optimize the chain-of-thought. Using GRPO, the model generates multiple candidate reasoning paths for each prompt. The candidate with the highest relative rewardassessed based on correctness, clarity, and formattingis selected and used for further training. Moreover, DeepSeek incorporates a self-reflection stage, where the model reviews its own generated reasoning and makes adjustments. This iterative process of generation, evaluation, and refinement leads to a more robust reasoning capability.

Benefits of Chain-of-Thought Modeling

Chain-of-thought modeling provides several key benefits:

- **Enhanced Transparency:** A model that articulates its reasoning steps allows users to understand and verify its thought process. This is especially important in domains where accountability and explainability are critical.

- **Improved Generalization:** By learning to reason step-by-step, the model is better equipped to handle novel or complex problems that were not explicitly encountered during training. This structured approach to problem-solving enables more reliable generalization.

- **Facilitation of Partial Credit:** In educational settings or diagnostic applications, even if the final answer is incorrect, a well-articulated reasoning process can provide valuable insights and earn partial credit.

- **Alignment with Human Processes:** Mimicking the human approach of showing ones work not only makes the models outputs more interpretable but also aligns its training with cognitive processes that humans use to solve problems.

77

- **Error Diagnosis and Debugging:** Detailed chains-of-thought make it easier to identify where errors occur in the reasoning process, facilitating more effective debugging and iterative improvement of the model.

Challenges and Trade-Offs

Despite its many advantages, chain-of-thought modeling also introduces challenges:

- **Increased Complexity:** Annotating training data with explicit reasoning steps and designing templates adds complexity to the data preparation process.

- **Computational Overhead:** Generating and evaluating multi-step reasoning processes can be more computationally intensive than producing a single output token, potentially increasing training time.

- **Reward Function Design:** Crafting a reward function that balances correctness, clarity, and format is non-trivial. Overemphasis on any single component can skew the models behavior, leading to overly verbose or excessively terse outputs.

- **Training Instability:** Integrating reinforcement learning into the training pipeline, especially with techniques like GRPO, can introduce instability if not carefully managed. Variability in reward signals may lead to oscillations or divergence if hyperparameters are not properly tuned.

- **Evaluation Difficulties:** Evaluating the quality of the reasoning process is inherently more subjective than evaluating a final answer. Developing objective metrics for clarity and logical coherence remains an active area of research.

The field of chain-of-thought modeling is rapidly evolving. Future research might explore:

- **Adaptive Templates:** Rather than relying on fixed templates, models could learn to adapt their reasoning format dynamically based on the task at hand.

- **Hybrid Training Strategies:** Combining supervised fine-tuning with reinforcement learning in a more integrated manner could further improve reasoning quality. For instance, selective application of RL to only the reasoning components of a model might reduce computational costs while maintaining output quality.

- **Enhanced Interpretability Tools:** Developing visualization techniques and interpretability frameworks to analyze the internal chain-of-thought can help researchers diagnose errors and improve the model.

- **Domain-Specific Process Modeling:** Tailoring chain-of-thought templates and reward functions for specific domains (e.g., legal, medical, scientific) could lead to more specialized and effective reasoning in those areas.

- **Interactive Human Feedback:** Incorporating real-time feedback from human users into the training loop could further align the models reasoning with human expectations, making the outputs even more reliable.

Chain-of-thought modeling represents a significant shift in the way LLMs are trained and evaluated. By moving from an output-centric approach to a process-centric one, models are not only judged on the correctness of their final answers but also on the clarity and logical structure of the steps they take to reach those answers. This paradigm fosters transparency, aids in error diagnosis, and leads to more robust generalizationqualities that are essential for real-world applications where trust and interpretability are paramount.

DeepSeek s implementation of chain-of-thought modeling exemplifies these principles. Through the use of explicit process markers, standardized templates, reflection and self-verification techniques, and the integration of reinforcement learning (via GRPO) with process supervision, DeepSeek has developed models capable of producing coherent and interpretable reasoning paths. These advancements contribute not only to better performance on complex tasks but also to a deeper alignment between machine-generated reasoning and human cognitive processes.

As we continue to push the boundaries of AI, chain-of-thought modeling will remain a critical area of research, driving innovations that make models more transparent, reliable, and ultimately more useful in diverse and challenging domains. This structured approach to reasoning is poised to transform how we evaluate and interact with AI systems, paving the way for models that not only provide answers but also explain the reasoning behind them in a clear, step-by-step manner.

Chapter 4

Pre-training Data and Corpus Curation

This chapter provides a detailed explanation of how DeepSeek curates, processes, and prepares its pre-training data to support the development of large language models capable of advanced reasoning, long-context understanding, and multi-domain competence. It covers the composition of DeepSeeks corpus, including general text, code, and math datasets, along with essential cleaning, formatting, and tokenization processes. By understanding DeepSeeks approach to data selection, quality control, and weighting strategies, expert readers gain the foundational knowledge needed to replicate DeepSeeks pre-training pipeline with high fidelity.

4.1 Composition of DeepSeeks Pre-training Corpus

The composition of the pre-training corpus is one of the most critical factors influencing the capabilities of a large language model (LLM). For DeepSeeks models, particularly DeepSeek-R1, the corpus was carefully curated to ensure balanced proficiency across general language understanding, programming knowledge, and advanced reasoning abilities. This section provides a detailed exploration of the types of data DeepSeek used, the rationale behind each data category, and how these diverse sources collectively shape the models capabilities.

Goals of Data Composition:

Every pre-training corpus reflects a series of design choices tied to the models intended use. In the case of DeepSeek, the overarching goals can be summarized as:

- Developing strong general-purpose linguistic fluency across multiple domains.

- Enabling advanced mathematical and logical reasoning through specialized training data.

- Building deep competence in programming and computational problem-solving.

- Supporting long-context understanding, with sequences up to 128K tokens.

Achieving these goals requires curating data that spans multiple modalities: natural language text, code, math problems, and reasoning-intensive content.

Core Data Sources:

DeepSeek s pre-training corpus integrates data from four primary categories, each serving a distinct purpose in shaping the models knowledge and skills. Table 4.1 summarizes these sources and their intended functions.

Category	Examples	Primary Purpose
General Language Data	Wikipedia, Books, Web Documents	Core language proficiency, factual knowledge
Programming Data	GitHub, CodeContests, StackOverflow	Coding knowledge, algorithmic thinking
Mathematical Reasoning	GSM8K, MATH, AIME, MATH500	Multi-step reasoning, formal logic
Long Documents	Full books, academic papers, multi-file projects	Long-context learning

Table 4.1: Primary Data Categories in DeepSeek Pre-training Corpus

General Language Data:

General web text forms the backbone of almost every LLMs training corpus. For DeepSeek, this includes standard sources such as:

- Wikipedia broad factual coverage across topics.

- Books long-form narrative and expository writing.

- Filtered web crawls diverse styles and domains.

This data ensures the model develops core fluency in grammar, semantics, and general knowledge retrieval, providing the baseline linguistic competence necessary for all downstream tasks.

Programming Data:

A unique emphasis in DeepSeeks corpus is programming and computational problem-solving data. This is especially critical for DeepSeek-Coder and DeepSeek-R1, both of which aim to excel in generating correct, executable code and solving algorithmic challenges. Programming data includes:

- Large-scale GitHub repositories covering diverse languages and paradigms.

- Competitive programming datasets such as CodeContests, which feature highly challenging algorithmic problems requiring logical precision.

- Developer Q&A from sources like StackOverflow, capturing real-world programming questions and solutions.

This component of the corpus teaches the model not only the syntax and semantics of programming languages but also best practices, debugging strategies, and real-world development patterns.

Mathematical and Reasoning Data:

The most distinctive aspect of DeepSeeks pre-training corpus is its heavy emphasis on mathematical and logical reasoning. Unlike general-purpose LLMs that train primarily on natural language text, DeepSeek-R1 is explicitly designed to excel in formal reasoning tasks. This requires substantial exposure to:

- Math problem datasets like GSM8K (grade-school word problems) and MATH (high school competition problems).

- Advanced math contests like AIME, which test multi-step reasoning under strict logical constraints.

- DeepSeeks own curated MATH500 dataset, created specifically to stress-test high-level mathematical reasoning.

- Codeforces problems, which blend algorithmic reasoning with practical coding.

These datasets teach the model to break down complex problems into manageable steps, apply formal rules consistently, and generate solutions that are both logically valid and computationally precise.

Long Documents and Long-Context Learning:

To support DeepSeeks 128K-token context length, the corpus includes large quantities of naturally long documents, including:

- Full-length books from Project Gutenberg and similar sources.

- Scientific papers, particularly in mathematics, physics, and computer science.

- Multi-file programming projects that require cross-file understanding.

Training on naturally long documents is superior to artificially concatenating short documents, as it preserves the natural long-range dependencies and discourse structures present in real-world data. This exposure is critical for enabling DeepSeek models to handle extended reasoning across large contexts, such as working through entire scientific papers or tracing logic across files in large codebases.

Corpus Balance and Weighting:

The proportion of each data type in the final corpus reflects the desired skill profile of the model. For example, general language data might form the majority of tokens for early stages of training, but reasoning and coding data receive progressively higher weights in later stages. Figure 4.1 illustrates a typical staged weighting strategy.

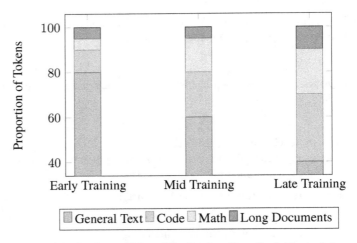

Figure 4.1: Evolving Token Mix During DeepSeek Pre-training

Domain-Specific and Specialized Content:

In addition to the core categories, DeepSeeks corpus also includes specialized content from:

- Scientific and technical papers.

- Legal documents (for structured legal reasoning).

- Multilingual text (for cross-lingual abilities, though this is less emphasized in DeepSeek-R1).

These specialized domains enrich the models ability to reason within technical, scientific, and formal contexts, extending its versatility beyond everyday conversational tasks.

Corpus Scale and Token Counts:

Though exact figures are rarely disclosed in full, public statements and typical scaling patterns for competitive LLMs suggest that DeepSeeks corpus spans several trillion tokens. Table 4.2 provides an estimated breakdown based on comparable open models.

85

Category	Estimated Tokens
General Text	3.5T
Code	1.0T
Math	300B
Long Documents	200B

Table 4.2: Estimated Token Counts in DeepSeek Pre-training Corpus

The composition of DeepSeeks pre-training corpus reflects a deliberate strategy to combine general-purpose language proficiency with domain-specialized reasoning skills. By blending web text, code, and curated mathematical content, DeepSeek ensures its models excel at both everyday language tasks and advanced problem-solving challenges. This carefully balanced corpus serves as the essential foundation upon which all other training techniquesfrom model architecture to fine-tuning and reinforcement learningare built.

4.2 Data Cleaning and Quality Filtering

The effectiveness of any large language model (LLM) is fundamentally linked to the quality of its pre-training data. Even the most sophisticated model architectures, optimization algorithms, and hardware infrastructure cannot compensate for poorly curated data. This is especially true for models like DeepSeek, which target not only general linguistic fluency but also advanced reasoning, mathematical competence, and coding accuracy. Achieving these goals requires a corpus free from irrelevant noise, duplication, and low-quality content. This section explains the techniques, processes, and theoretical reasoning behind the data cleaning and quality filtering pipeline essential for replicating DeepSeeks pre-training data preparation.

The Importance of Data Cleaning.

Raw data collected from public web crawls, code repositories, and reasoning datasets is far from ready for direct use in LLM training. It often contains noise such as:

- Duplicate documents appearing multiple times across different sites.

- Low-information content, including boilerplate web pages, navigation menus, and SEO spam.

- Encoding errors, broken formatting, and incomplete documents.

- Inconsistent formatting, especially in math and code data.

Training on noisy data wastes compute, reduces model efficiency, and leads to degraded performance on both general tasks and specialized reasoning benchmarks. Quality filtering is essential not only for optimizing training efficiency but also for ensuring the model learns the correct distribution of high-quality reasoning steps, coding practices, and mathematical logic.

Typical Data Cleaning Pipeline.

A standard LLM data cleaning pipeline consists of multiple stages, each addressing a different type of quality issue. Figure 4.2 visualizes a typical process.

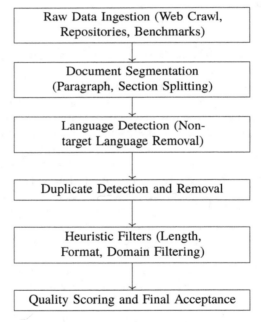

Figure 4.2: Overview of a Data Cleaning Pipeline

Exact and Near-Duplicate Removal.

87

Duplicate documents waste training capacity and bias the model toward over-represented content. Deduplication occurs at two levels:

- **Exact duplicates**: Documents or files identical across all tokens.

- **Near duplicates**: Documents that differ only slightly, such as minor formatting changes or slight edits.

For exact deduplication, simple hashing (e.g., SHA256) suffices. For near-duplicates, techniques like MinHash, SimHash, or embedding-based similarity search are applied. In code datasets, deduplication is even more critical, as popular repositories (like sorting algorithm implementations) are cloned thousands of times. Figure 4.3 illustrates the effect of deduplication on reducing redundancy in a code corpus.

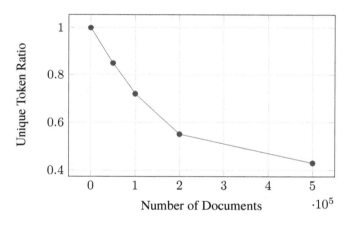

Figure 4.3: Decline in Unique Token Ratio with Increasing Corpus Size (Without Deduplication)

Length and Structural Filtering.

Documents that are too short (single sentence fragments, empty files) or excessively long (logs or dumps) are filtered. Typical length thresholds:

- Minimum: 100 tokens.

- Maximum: 200K tokens (for books or multi-file concatenated projects).

88

For code data, files dominated by boilerplate headers, licenses, or auto-generated comments are also excluded.

Language Identification.

For multilingual corpora, language detection ensures that only content in the desired languages (e.g., English, Chinese) passes through. This is commonly done using tools like `langdetect` or `fastText`. Ambiguous cases (low-confidence classification) are discarded to avoid contamination.

Heuristic and Rule-Based Filters.

DeepSeek -like pipelines also employ domain-specific heuristics. Examples:

- Removing pages with abnormal character distributions (too many non-ASCII symbols in English data).

- Discarding documents with excessive boilerplate (menus, copyright notices).

- Filtering out low-information content, e.g., cookie banners.

For math and code, ensuring files contain valid syntactic structures (well-formed equations, compilable code) is particularly important.

Document Quality Scoring.

Beyond simple rule-based filters, more advanced pipelines apply trained quality models to estimate content usefulness. Quality models can be trained to distinguish:

- High-quality prose vs keyword-stuffed spam.

- Well-documented code vs poorly commented, incomprehensible scripts.

- Mathematically correct solutions vs erroneous ones.

These models output scores that help prioritize inclusion during data selection.

Case Study: Math Dataset Cleaning.

Mathematical datasets used by DeepSeek receive special handling:

- Ensure all problems have complete statements and answers.

- Preserve step-by-step solutions where available.

- Check for consistent formatting of symbols and equations (e.g., LaTeX rendering issues).

This ensures reasoning problems present a clear, logically valid process for the model to learn from.

Balancing Recall and Precision in Filtering.

Overly aggressive filtering risks losing rare, valuable data (e.g., specialized mathematical proofs). Under-filtering allows noise and low-quality content to dilute training. Effective pipelines optimize this trade-off by:

- Using permissive filters initially (high recall).

- Applying stricter quality scoring at the final selection stage (high precision).

This staged approach preserves maximum signal while removing harmful noise.

Quality Feedback Loops During Training.

The cleaning pipeline is not static. During early pre-training stages, perplexity analysis reveals:

- Unexpected difficult documents (indicating low-quality data).

- Unexpected easy documents (indicating redundant or overly simple data).

These signals feed back into the cleaning pipeline, gradually improving corpus quality for future training runs.

Pre-training success depends not only on raw data volume but also on rigorous quality control. DeepSeeks data cleaning pipeline reflects best practices from the broader LLM community, enhanced with domain-specific strategies for reasoning and code data. By combining deduplication, structural filtering, content scoring, and iterative feedback, the pipeline ensures that DeepSeek models learn from data that is clean, diverse, and well-matched to the reasoning challenges they are designed to solve.

4.3 Training Techniques and Dataset Curation (14.8 Trillion Tokens)

The pre-training of DeepSeek-V3 represents a large-scale undertaking, characterized by the meticulous curation of a 14.8 trillion token dataset and the deployment of advanced training methodologies. This dataset, sourced from a diverse range of domains and languages, forms the bedrock for the model's comprehensive linguistic understanding. This section details the dataset curation strategies, including rigorous cleaning and deduplication procedures, and elucidates the innovative training techniques employed to achieve stable and efficient learning at this scale.

Dataset Curation: A 14.8 Trillion Token Corpus

The DeepSeek-V3 model is pre-trained on a massive dataset comprising 14.8 trillion tokens. This corpus is meticulously assembled from a wide array of sources to ensure linguistic diversity and comprehensive coverage. Data sources include:

- **Traditional Textual Sources:** Books, academic publications, and news media.

- **Web Content:** Data extracted from diverse websites, social media platforms, and online forums.

- **Technical and Specialized Domains:** Technical documentation, scientific literature, code repositories, and expert Q&A datasets.

This multi-faceted data sourcing strategy ensures that the training corpus encompasses a broad spectrum of linguistic styles, topical domains, and cultural contexts, which is crucial for the model's generalization capabilities across diverse downstream tasks.

Rigorous Data Preparation and Refinement

Data preparation for DeepSeek-V3 involves a multi-stage refinement process to ensure high quality and eliminate redundancy. Key steps include:

1. **Iterative Dataset Refinement:** An iterative approach to enhance data quality through multiple cycles of refinement:

    - *Deduplication:* Aggressive near-duplicate detection and removal to eliminate redundant content.

91

- *Filtering:* Linguistic and semantic assessments to ensure high document quality at individual and global levels, removing low-quality domains and content.

- *Remixing:* Dataset balancing by incorporating content from underrepresented domains to enhance inclusivity and diversity.

2. **Bias Identification and Mitigation:** Procedures to identify and mitigate subjective biases related to cultural or regional values. This involves manual analysis of model underperformance in specific areas and removal or adjustment of contentious content.

3. **Language and Domain Classification:** Natural Language Processing (NLP) classifiers are used to tag data points with language and domain labels, enabling balanced representation during training and preventing over-dominance of specific languages or topics.

These rigorous curation steps ensure that the 14.8 trillion token dataset is not only massive in scale but also of high quality and diversity, providing a robust foundation for pre-training.

Advanced Training Techniques for Scalability and Efficiency

DeepSeek -V3 employs a suite of advanced training techniques to effectively leverage its large-scale dataset and model architecture, ensuring both scalability and training efficiency:

- **Multi-Token Prediction (MTP):** Instead of predicting only the next token, DeepSeek-V3 utilizes a multi-token prediction objective. This technique trains the model to predict multiple tokens concurrently, enhancing training efficiency and improving text generation fluency, particularly for code and math-related tasks. MTP also facilitates speculative decoding for accelerated inference. DeepSeek-V3 employs a sequential MTP approach with shared embedding and output layers, incorporating specialized MTP modules to predict future tokens based on current token representations.

- **FP8 Mixed Precision Training:** To manage computational demands and reduce memory footprint, DeepSeek-V3 employs FP8 mixed-precision training. This framework conducts most compute-intensive operations in FP8, while maintaining critical computations in higher precision (BF16 or FP32) for numerical stability. DeepSeek-V3 utilizes fine-grained quantization methods, including tile-wise and block-wise grouping with dynamic scaling, to address challenges of underflow, overflow, and quantization errors inherent in FP8 training. This approach achieves significant reductions in memory usage (over 50%) and computational cost, enabling efficient training of the 671B parameter model.

- **DualPipe Parallelism for Distributed Training:** DeepSeek-V3 leverages a cluster of 2048 H800 GPUs, employing "DualPipe" parallelism to optimize distributed training. DualPipe is a pipeline parallelism algorithm designed to maximize computation-communication overlap, reducing GPU idle time and improving overall efficiency. Combined with InfiniBand high-speed communication and NVLink, DualPipe facilitates efficient cross-node parameter synchronization, enabling stable and scalable training across a large GPU cluster.

- **Stable Training Optimization:** To ensure training stability at scale, DeepSeek-V3 employs careful optimization settings, including adaptive gradient methods and tailored learning rate schedules with a warm-up and decay phase. These strategies prevent loss spikes and maintain a smooth training trajectory, crucial for convergence in large MoE models.

DeepSeek -V3's training paradigm is notable for its efficiency and cost-effectiveness. The model was pre-trained on 14.8 trillion tokens using approximately 2.788 million H800 GPU hours, at an estimated cost of around $5.6 million USD. This efficiency is attributed to the synergistic combination of architectural innovations (MoE with MLA), auxiliary-loss-free load balancing, multi-token prediction, and FP8 mixed-precision training, along with optimized distributed training infrastructure. The remarkably stable training process, devoid of irrecoverable loss spikes or rollbacks, further underscores the robustness of DeepSeek-V3's training methodology.

The training of DeepSeek-V3 exemplifies a holistic and innovative approach to large language model development. The expansive and meticulously curated 14.8 trillion token dataset, combined with advanced training techniques such as multi-token prediction, FP8 mixed precision, and DualPipe parallelism, establishes a new benchmark for training large-scale LLMs. This comprehensive strategy not only enables DeepSeek-V3 to achieve state-of-the-art performance but also demonstrates a pathway to scaling language models efficiently and cost-effectively, paving the way for future advancements in the field. The emphasis on both data quality and algorithmic innovation in DeepSeek-V3's training process highlights a paradigm shift towards more sustainable and scalable large language model development.

4.4   Formatting and Tokenization

The process of formatting and tokenization serves as the final transformation stage between raw pre-training data and the sequences consumed by the language model during training. This step defines how every word, symbol, equation, and programming statement is represented numerically. For large language models (LLMs) like DeepSeek, proper tokenization is more than a preprocessing detail—it directly influences learning efficiency, reasoning capacity, and even downstream performance on specialized tasks. A model cannot effectively reason about mathematical notation, programming logic, or step-wise reasoning processes unless its tokenizer faithfully preserves these structures.

Tokenization splits raw text into smaller units called tokens, which are then mapped to integer indices in a fixed-size vocabulary. This allows language models to process sequences of numbers rather than characters or words directly. For DeepSeek, which handles general text, code, and mathematical reasoning, tokenization must balance several competing goals:

- Efficiently compress common words and symbols into single tokens.

- Preserve fine-grained distinctions for rare, technical terms (especially in code and math).

- Support reasoning-specific formatting such as labeled steps, intermediate reflections, and logic chains.

The choice of tokenization method influences how much context fits into a given window (measured in tokens), how fast training proceeds, and how well the model handles non-standard text.

Byte Pair Encoding (BPE) DeepSeek uses **Byte Pair Encoding (BPE)**, a subword tokenization method that strikes a balance between a compact representation of common terms and flexibility to handle rare words. BPE iteratively merges the most common adjacent character pairs into new symbols, eventually forming a vocabulary of fixed size. This makes it particularly effective for morphologically rich languages, mathematical expressions, and programming syntax.

The BPE process can be visualized as follows:

Step	Corpus Representation
Initial	`natural language processing`
Split into characters	`n a t u r a l l a n g u a g e p r o c e s s i n g`
Merge frequent pairs	`natural language processing` (back to words)

Table 4.3: Example Process of Byte Pair Encoding

For models like DeepSeek, trained on multilingual text, code, and math, BPE is trained on a **balanced sample** from all domains. This ensures no domain (e.g., natural language vs. code) dominates tokenization behavior.

Vocabulary Size and Token Granularity DeepSeek 's tokenizer uses a vocabulary size of approximately 100,000 tokens, balancing:

- Sufficient granularity to handle diverse languages, including technical and mathematical notation.

- Efficiency to minimize average sequence length in tokens.

This vocabulary size is larger than that of general-purpose models like GPT-2 (50,000 tokens) to account for DeepSeeks focus on code and reasoning data, which contain many rare symbols and multi-character operators.

Special Formatting for Different Data Types DeepSeek 's corpus spans multiple domains, each requiring tailored formatting rules before tokenization.

General Text.

- Standard plain text with minimal preprocessing.

- Minor normalization (unifying quotes, standardizing dashes).

Code.

- Preserves indentation to retain block structure.

95

- Keeps special symbols intact ({, }, =>, etc.).

- Ensures that comments, docstrings, and metadata are correctly formatted to retain programming context.

Math.

- Converts all math content to a consistent LaTeX-like format.

- Ensures mathematical symbols map directly to individual tokens where possible (e.g., π, $\sqrt{}$, $\int$).

- Cleans up OCR errors or alternate math notations (e.g., replacing sqrt() with \sqrt{}).

Reasoning Chains.

- Inserts process markers such as:

```
<think> Step 1: Define variables </think>
```

- Treats these tags as atomic tokens in the final vocabulary, ensuring they are preserved during processing and generation.

Reasoning Tags and Process Annotation A distinctive feature of DeepSeek's training corpus is its use of **reasoning process tags**. These explicitly indicate:

- Logical step progression.

- Reflection and verification points.

- Intermediate thoughts and subgoals.

For example:

```
<think> First, I will define the variables. </think>
<think> Next, I substitute values into the equation. </think>
```

Treating these tags as single tokens ensures:

96

- The reasoning structure is preserved even if tokenization splits the surrounding text.

- The model can easily identify, generate, and interpret reasoning steps.

Long-Context Handling During Tokenization DeepSeek supports context lengths up to 128K tokens. When documents exceed this length, they must be split. This is not simply truncation; to preserve logical and semantic continuity across splits, DeepSeek applies:

- Overlapping context windows (e.g., 50-token overlap between segments).

- Continuation markers such as:

```
<cont> Continued from previous segment. </cont>
```

- This helps the model retain memory across long spans, especially in math proofs or multi-file code projects.

Mathematical Expression Handling Mathematical expressions, especially in competition math datasets (AIME, MATH500), pose unique tokenization challenges:

- Ensure operators (e.g., +, *,̂) are individual tokens.

- Handle multi-character symbols (e.g., \sqrt{}) as atomic units.

- Preserve correct nesting for fractions, integrals, matrices.

This is handled via pre-standardization, where all math content is normalized into a canonical LaTeX-inspired format before tokenization.

Vocabulary Coverage Analysis Once tokenization is complete, it is essential to check:

- Average sequence length across domains.

- Percentage of terms fully covered versus split into multiple tokens.

- Out-of-vocabulary (OOV) rate for each data type.

Table 4.4 illustrates a hypothetical vocabulary coverage report for DeepSeek's corpus.

Domain	Avg Tokens/Doc	Single-Token Coverage	OOV Rate
General Text	1,200	94%	0.5%
Code	3,500	88%	1.5%
Math	800	82%	3.2%
Reasoning (with tags)	1,000	89%	2.1%

Table 4.4: Vocabulary Coverage Statistics Across Domains

Training a Custom Tokenizer To replicate DeepSeek's training pipeline, readers should:

- Collect a representative sample of the corpus.

- Use a standard BPE training tool (like SentencePiece).

- Set vocabulary size (e.g., 100K tokens).

- Predefine certain tokens (reasoning tags, math operators) to be atomic.

Sample command:

```
spm_train --input=corpus.txt --model_prefix=deepseek_bpe \
--vocab_size=100000 --character_coverage=1.0
```

Correct tokenization is one of the most underestimated aspects of large-scale language model replication. For DeepSeek, preserving reasoning structure, code formatting, and mathematical notation is essential to maintaining the model's reasoning capabilities. By combining domain-specific formatting rules, special token handling, and customized BPE training, DeepSeek ensures its models learn from high-quality, logically structured input—the foundation of their exceptional performance on reasoning and coding tasks.

4.5 Dataset Balancing and Weighting

The composition of a pre-training corpus for a large language model (LLM) is not simply a matter of collecting a vast quantity of data. Each type of datawhether general text, code, or mathematical reasoning problemsimparts

98

different skills to the model. Controlling the *balance* between these sources is critical to shaping the final models capabilities. DeepSeeks exceptional performance in reasoning-centric tasks stems not just from the quality of its data but also from the deliberate and evolving choices about *how much* of each type of data to expose the model to during training. This section details the strategies used to balance DeepSeeks training corpus and explains how expert readers can design their own weighting pipelines for replication.

Why Dataset Balancing Matters

At the heart of LLM training lies a fundamental trade-off: different types of data promote different competencies. If pre-training is dominated by general web text, the model develops broad factual knowledge and conversational fluency. However, if reasoning-intensive data (math problems, algorithmic challenges) is underrepresented, the model will struggle with multi-step logical inference.

The influence of dataset balance can be visualized as a performance trade-off triangle, shown in Figure 4.4. Emphasizing one axis (e.g., conversational fluency) may come at the expense of others (e.g., deep reasoning or formal precision).

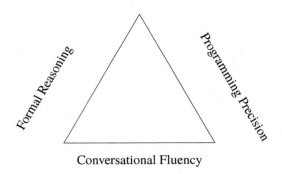

Figure 4.4: The Performance Trade-off Triangle Influenced by Dataset Balancing

For general-purpose models like GPT-3 or LLaMA, the balance heavily favors general text. DeepSeek, in contrast, specifically shifted toward reasoning and programming data, resulting in models particularly adept at solving math and logic problems.

99

DeepSeek s Multi-Domain Data Sources

DeepSeek s corpus spans several major categories, each with its own educational value:

- **General Text**: Books, Wikipedia, filtered web documents.

- **Programming Data**: GitHub repositories, competitive programming solutions.

- **Mathematical and Reasoning Data**: GSM8K, MATH, AIME, MATH500.

- **Long Documents**: Full books, academic papers, multi-file codebases.

Each domain contributes to different aspects of the final models skill set, shown in Table 4.5.

Data Domain	Primary Contribution
General Text	Fluency, factual knowledge, commonsense reasoning
Programming	Syntax mastery, algorithmic thinking, procedural logic
Math/Reasoning	Multi-step inference, formal logic, symbolic reasoning
Long Documents	Discourse coherence, cross-section reference ability

Table 4.5: Skill Contributions from Different Data Sources

Fixed Proportion vs Curriculum Balancing

Two primary strategies exist for balancing datasets during training:

- **Fixed Proportion**: Every training batch contains a constant ratio of text, code, and math samples.

- **Curriculum Balancing**: The data mixture evolves over time, starting with simpler, general content and gradually increasing the proportion of harder reasoning data.

DeepSeek s training likely followed a curriculum schedule resembling Figure 4.5, starting with general text to establish fluency, then gradually introducing more math and programming to sharpen reasoning.

100

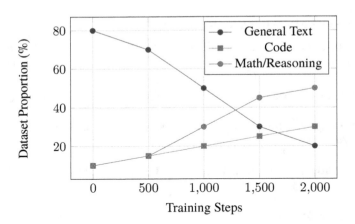

Figure 4.5: Hypothetical Curriculum Balancing Schedule for DeepSeek-R1

Upsampling Specialized Reasoning Datasets

A critical aspect of DeepSeeks balance is the deliberate upsampling of *reasoning benchmarks* like GSM8K and MATH500. These datasets represent only a small fraction of the raw corpus but are extremely important for final performance on DeepSeeks reasoning tasks. To ensure the model sees them frequently, they are over-sampled relative to their natural occurrence.

This can be implemented programmatically:

```
sources = ["general", "code", "math"]
weights = [0.4, 0.3, 0.3] # during late-stage training
source = random.choices(sources, weights=weights)[0]
```

This guarantees every training batch contains a nontrivial amount of reasoning data.

Within-Domain Weighting

Even within a single data type, balancing matters:

- Programming: Popular languages (Python, JavaScript) vs niche languages (Fortran, COBOL).

- Math: Simple arithmetic vs advanced proofs.

- Reasoning: Short 3-step problems vs multi-page derivations.

101

DeepSeek likely applied some intra-domain weighting to ensure adequate exposure to both simple and complex problems, avoiding overfitting to just one class of reasoning.

Balancing Evaluation Signals

Dataset balance is also informed by continuous evaluation during training. If the model performs poorly on math benchmarks mid-training, the pipeline can respond by temporarily increasing math data sampling a form of *adaptive curriculum*. This creates a dynamic feedback loop between pre-training performance and dataset weighting.

Long-Context Documents

To train DeepSeek for long-context reasoning (up to 128K tokens), long documents receive a stable proportion in every batch, ensuring the model continuously practices processing and understanding long-form content. These documents are sampled directly rather than artificially concatenated, preserving natural discourse structure.

Balancing Challenges and Trade-offs

Overemphasizing any single domain risks:

- Domain overfitting (e.g., math-rich models losing conversational fluency).

- Poor generalization to unseen tasks (overfitting to specific reasoning templates).

Balancing is thus an *iterative optimization process*, continually refined based on evaluation feedback and final task performance.

Dataset balancing and weighting play a foundational role in shaping a models capabilities. DeepSeeks success at reasoning-intensive tasks stems directly from its carefully curated balance between general fluency data, programming challenges, mathematical problems, and long-context documents. Replicating DeepSeeks performance requires not only collecting similar data but also closely mimicking its evolutionary curriculum ensuring the model sees the right data, at the right time, in the right proportions.

Chapter 5

Model Training Pipeline

This chapter presents the core training pipeline required to replicate DeepSeeks model development process, covering the essential technical steps from data streaming to distributed training and optimization. It explains how DeepSeek manages large-scale data loading, initializes its transformer architecture, applies mixed precision and memory-saving techniques, and coordinates parallel training across multiple GPUs. By understanding the optimization algorithms, loss tracking, and real-time evaluation methods used during training, expert readers gain a complete view of the processes needed to train DeepSeek-like models efficiently and reliably.

5.1   Preparing the Data Pipeline

The data pipeline is the first operational stage in the training process of a large language model (LLM). While Chapter 4 covered how the pre-training corpus is collected, cleaned, and tokenized, this section focuses on the engineering pipeline responsible for efficiently feeding that data into the training system itself. For DeepSeek-scale trainingwhere thousands of GPUs operate in parallelthis pipeline must deliver token batches continuously, with minimal stalls, while preserving the intended data mixture, document structure, and sequence packing. This section outlines the techniques, formats, and performance optimizations required to build such a pipeline.

From Cleaned Data to Training Batches. Once the data corpus is fully curated and tokenized, it exists in the form of token sequences, typically grouped into documents. These documents must be divided into shards that can be distributed across worker nodes in a training cluster. Each worker reads, shuffles, and batches its assigned shard, producing sequences that match the models expected input size, such as 4,096 or 128,000 tokens.

Storing Pre-processed Data Efficiently. Raw text files are unsuitable for efficient streaming into GPUs at scale. Instead, pre-processed data is typically stored in binary formats optimized for sequential reading. Common choices include:

- **TFRecord** Originally from TensorFlow, widely used for sharded binary data.

- **Arrow** Columnar format designed for fast access.

- **Custom binary formats** Many LLM teams build their own, optimized for token sequences.

Each shard might contain thousands of tokenized documents, with metadata indicating boundaries, document types, and any special tags such as reasoning markers.

Sharding and Distribution. The corpus is split into multiple shards, typically one per worker. A cluster of 1,024 GPUs might operate with 256 nodes, each handling 4 GPUs, so the corpus would be split into at least 256 shards, with replication to guard against node failures. Each shard should contain a representative sample of all data types (general text, code, math), preserving the intended data balance.

Shard ID	Document Count	Domains Covered
Shard 0	10,000	Text, Code, Math
Shard 1	10,000	Text, Code, Math
⋮	⋮	⋮

Table 5.1: Example Shard Metadata

Shuffling Strategies. Shuffling is critical to prevent training artifacts caused by domain clumping (where batches contain only math or only code). Shuffling happens at two levels:

104

- **Global Shuffling**: Performed once across the entire corpus before sharding.

- **Per-Shard Shuffling**: Each worker re-shuffles its shard every epoch.

Global shuffling ensures domain mixing across the corpus, while per-shard shuffling handles local randomness within each node.

Batch Packing and Sequence Formation. Since DeepSeek-R1 supports up to 128K tokens per sequence, efficiently packing documents into those sequences is crucial to minimize wasted padding. Common strategies include:

- **Document Packing**: Multiple short documents packed into a single sequence.

- **Padding Minimization**: Precompute packing layouts to minimize pad tokens.

An example packing might look like:

$$[\text{Doc}_1, \text{PAD}, \text{Doc}_2, \text{Doc}_3, \text{PAD}]$$

Special boundary tokens (e.g., `<doc_sep>`) help the model distinguish between documents.

Handling Long Documents. Some documents (books, papers) exceed even 128K tokens. These require:

- **Sliding Window Splits**: Divide the document into overlapping windows, preserving coherence across boundaries.

- **Continuation Markers**: Insert tokens like `<cont>` to signal that a new segment is a continuation of the same document.

For example, a 300K token book could be split into:

$$\text{Chunk}_1 = [\text{Start}, \ldots, 128\text{K tokens}]$$

$$\text{Chunk}_2 = [\text{cont}, \ldots, 128\text{K tokens}]$$

Pre-fetching and Streaming Optimization. To avoid starving the GPUs during training, each worker maintains a *prefetch queue* that loads future batches in the background while the current batch trains. Common pre-fetching optimizations include:

105

- Asynchronous I/O using dedicated data loader threads.

- Pinning memory to avoid page faults during transfer.

- Caching frequently accessed documents in RAM for reuse.

Figure 5.1: Simplified Data Pipeline

Format Alignment with Model Inputs. Each training batch is ultimately a structured object fed into the model. In the case of DeepSeek, batches contain:

- Token IDs (integer tensor of shape [batch size, sequence length]).

- Attention Masks (binary tensor masking padded positions).

- Expert Routing Information (for MoE models, indicating which tokens go to which experts).

This alignment ensures that data feeding and model computation fit seamlessly.

MoE-Specific Batch Handling. In mixture-of-experts models, each token is dynamically routed to a subset of model experts. This requires:

- Computing expert scores for each token.

- Generating expert assignment masks.

If routing is learned jointly with the model, this occurs inside the transformer block. If precomputed routing is used (e.g., from external classifiers), routing maps are part of the data pipeline itself.

Parallel Data Loading in Multi-Node Training. In distributed training, every node loads its own data shard, but global synchronization ensures:

- All nodes apply the same global shuffle seed.

- Validation/test sets are identical across all nodes.

106

This synchronization can be implemented using:

```
np.random.seed(global_seed + worker_rank)
```

This ensures shuffling remains globally consistent, preserving deterministic evaluation.

Quality Control During Data Loading. During initial training, the pipeline logs:

- Average tokens per batch (checking packing efficiency).

- Fraction of padding (high padding = wasted capacity).

- Domain distribution per batch (ensuring balanced sampling works correctly).

A sample log might look like:

```
[Batch 1045] tokens=128000 padding=3.2% text=45% code=30% math=25%
```

The data pipeline is the unsung workhorse of LLM training, quietly ensuring GPUs receive a steady supply of high-quality data in the right format and sequence structure. DeepSeeks ability to train reasoning-focused models at scale depends not just on good data, but on a *high-performance pipeline* that respects document boundaries, preserves reasoning tags, packs sequences efficiently, and streams continuously across thousands of GPUs. A well-designed data pipeline is not just a technical detailit is an essential foundation for successful model replication.

5.2 Model Initialization

The initialization of a large language model (LLM) defines the starting point from which all learning begins. Proper initialization is critical to ensure stable training, avoid early divergence, and provide a balanced learning environment for all components of the model. In the case of DeepSeek-R1, which incorporates a combination of standard transformer layers and Mixture-of-Experts (MoE) blocks, the initialization process must not only prepare traditional transformer weights, but also account for expert routing, embedding consistency, and positional encoding requirements. This section covers the essential processes and considerations required to correctly initialize a DeepSeek-like model.

Overview of the DeepSeek-R1 Architecture

DeepSeek -R1 follows a *decoder-only* transformer design with 64 layers. Each layer contains:

- Multi-head self-attention.

- A feedforward block, some of which are implemented as Mixture-of-Experts (MoE) layers.

The model has a total parameter count of 671 billion, though only 37 billion are active at any given time due to the sparse activation of MoE layers. The vocabulary size is approximately 100,000 tokens, and the maximum context length is 128,000 tokens. Positional information is handled using rotary positional embeddings (RoPE), which are dynamically applied at runtime rather than learned.

Weight Initialization for Standard Layers

For layers outside of the MoE structure (attention heads, non-expert feedforward paths), DeepSeek-R1 follows common transformer initialization practices. These include:

- **Xavier Initialization** (also known as Glorot Initialization) for linear layers.

- Initializing biases to zero in attention and feedforward layers.

- Scaling attention projection matrices based on the number of attention heads.

Xavier Initialization, derived from the assumption that activations should maintain consistent variance across layers, is defined as:

$$W \sim \mathcal{U}\left(-\sqrt{\frac{6}{d_{\text{in}} + d_{\text{out}}}}, \sqrt{\frac{6}{d_{\text{in}} + d_{\text{out}}}}\right)$$

This balances weight magnitudes according to input and output sizes, ensuring activations neither explode nor vanish at initialization.

Embedding Initialization

108

The input embedding matrix maps each token to a high-dimensional vector in the model's embedding space. This matrix must:

- Match the tokenizers vocabulary size.

- Use the same embeddings for input and output layers (known as *tied embeddings*) to reduce parameter count.

The embeddings are typically initialized with a normal distribution:

$$E_{i,j} \sim \mathcal{N}(0, \sigma^2)$$

where $\sigma = \frac{1}{\sqrt{d}}$ and d is the embedding dimension.

Positional Encoding: Rotary Embeddings

DeepSeek -R1 employs Rotary Positional Embeddings (RoPE), which do not require a learnable embedding table. Instead, RoPE computes position-dependent rotation matrices applied directly to query and key vectors during attention calculations. This rotation preserves absolute positional information while allowing graceful extrapolation to longer contexts.

The rotational matrix for position p and dimension d is given by:

$$\theta_k = \frac{10000^{-2k/d}}{128000}$$

This rotation is applied directly:

$$\mathbf{q}_p^{(k)} = \cos(p\theta_k)\, \mathbf{q}^{(k)} + \sin(p\theta_k)\, \mathbf{q}^{(k+1)}$$

Because this process is fully deterministic, no positional embeddings need to be stored in the model's parameters. This reduces initialization complexity and guarantees position handling is consistent across reinitializations.

Initializing Mixture-of-Experts (MoE) Layers

MoE layers introduce additional complexity. Each MoE block contains:

- A set of feedforward experts (typically 128 experts in DeepSeek-R1).

- A router network that assigns tokens to a small subset of these experts.

Each expert is initialized similarly to standard feedforward layers using Xavier Initialization. However, the router weightsresponsible for expert selectionrequire specialized treatment.

Router Initialization

The router maps token representations to expert selection probabilities:

$$r = \text{softmax}(W_{\text{router}}x + b_{\text{router}})$$

Special Token Initialization

DeepSeek models rely on a few special tokens, including:

- Padding token.

- Reasoning tags such as `<think>` and `<proof>`.

- Continuation markers for split long documents.

These tokens receive either random embeddings from the same initialization distribution as normal tokens or predefined embeddings if preserving special formatting (like the `<think>` structure) is critical.

Configuration File Example

```
{
    "num_layers": 64,
    "hidden_size": 8192,
    "num_heads": 64,
    "vocab_size": 100000,
    "max_position_embeddings": 128000,
    "moe": {
        "num_experts": 128,
        "top_k": 2
    },
    "position_embedding_type": "rope"
}
```

This file acts as the source of truth for both model construction and initialization.

Scaling Adjustments for Deep Models

For very deep transformers (over 60 layers), additional rescaling may be applied to attention and feedforward weights to maintain numerical stability:

$$W = \frac{W}{\sqrt{2L}}$$

110

where L is the number of layers. This keeps gradients well-conditioned in deep models, reducing the risk of gradient explosion or collapse.

Embedding Weight Tying

As is standard in large language models, DeepSeek ties the input embedding matrix E to the output projection matrix used to compute next-token logits. This reduces the total parameter count and enforces consistent token representations across input and output. The final logits for token prediction are computed as:

$$\text{logits} = E^T h + b$$

where h is the final hidden state.

Initialization Verification

```
print(f"Embedding Norm: {model.embeddings.weight.norm().item():.4f}")
print(f"Attention Weight Norm: {model.layers[0].self_attn.qkv_proj.weight.norm().
    item():.4f}")
print(f"Router Bias Mean: {model.moe_layers[0].router.bias.mean().item():.4f}")
```

These checks confirm that all critical weights are within expected ranges, and no accidental overwrites or mis-scalings have occurred.

Model initialization is more than a bookkeeping stepit defines the numerical landscape on which all future training occurs. For DeepSeek-R1, careful attention to transformer weight initialization, expert balancing in MoE, special token handling, and rotary positional encoding ensures stable early training, avoids expert collapse, and maintains compatibility with the tokenization process covered earlier. Reproducibility depends heavily on matching these initial conditions, making proper initialization essential to any serious attempt at replication.

5.3 Distributed Training Infrastructure

Training DeepSeek-R1, a model with 671 billion parameters, across thousands of GPUs requires an exceptionally efficient distributed training infrastructure. No single GPU or even a small cluster of machines can hold a model of this size entirely in memory. Consequently, DeepSeek relies on a combination of distributed training techniques, collectively referred to as hybrid parallelism, to split the model, the data, and the computational work across many GPUs. This section explains the essential methods employed, providing expert readers with the knowledge necessary to design and operate a comparable distributed training pipeline.

Why Distributed Training is Essential

The scale of DeepSeek-R1 places it firmly within the category of models that exceed any single hardware units capacity:

- The model weights alone exceed 2 terabytes in size.

- Processing 128K token sequences at reasonable batch sizes requires multiple terabytes of GPU memory for activations.

- Efficient training requires batch sizes large enough to stabilize optimization dynamics, which further inflates memory requirements.

Given these realities, distributing both the model and data across thousands of GPUs is not optionalit is fundamental to enabling training at all.

Parallelism Strategies

There are four principal forms of parallelism employed in DeepSeeks distributed infrastructure:

Data Parallelism. In data parallelism (DP), each GPU processes a unique slice of the training data while holding a full copy of the models parameters. After each training step, gradients from all GPUs are averaged across the cluster and applied uniformly to all parameter copies.

$$\theta \leftarrow \theta - \eta \cdot \frac{1}{N} \sum_{i=1}^{N} g_i$$

where g_i is the gradient computed on the ith GPU.

While simple and widely used, pure data parallelism is insufficient for models as large as DeepSeek-R1. Even a single layer of the model exceeds the memory capacity of modern GPUs, rendering data parallelism alone impractical.

Tensor Parallelism. Tensor parallelism (TP) addresses the memory bottleneck by **splitting each individual layer across multiple GPUs**. Each GPU holds only a slice of the weight matrices, and computations (like matrix multiplications) are split accordingly. This requires communication between GPUs

112

after every matrix multiplication step.

$$Y = XW = \sum_{i=1}^{P} XW_i$$

where P is the number of tensor-parallel slices.

Tensor parallelism is especially effective in attention layers, where large projection matrices dominate memory consumption. However, TP increases communication overhead, requiring careful tuning of GPU-to-GPU transfers to avoid stalls.

Pipeline Parallelism. Pipeline parallelism (PP) splits the model *vertically* across layers. One subset of GPUs holds the lower layers, another holds the middle layers, and so on. Each batch of data flows sequentially through these partitions, like cars moving through an assembly line.

$$y = f_4(f_3(f_2(f_1(x))))$$

where f_i denotes different groups of layers, each handled by a distinct GPU partition.

This approach allows very deep models to be split across many devices, though it introduces pipeline bubblesperiods where some GPUs are idle while waiting for upstream batches to complete. Pipeline bubbles can be reduced by breaking each batch into micro-batches that flow concurrently.

Expert Parallelism. For MoE layers, even tensor-parallel GPUs cannot store all experts. Instead, experts are themselves sharded across GPUs. During training, each token is dynamically assigned to a small subset of experts (typically 2 out of 128 in DeepSeek-R1). These assignments trigger **targeted inter-GPU communication**, where token activations flow to the responsible expert GPUs.

$$h_{\text{output}} = \sum_{k \in \text{SelectedExperts}} \pi_k \cdot E_k(h_{\text{input}})$$

where E_k denotes the kth expert and π_k is its router-assigned weight.

Combining Parallelism: Hybrid Parallelism in DeepSeek

DeepSeek -R1 combines these techniques into a **hybrid parallelism strategy**:

- **Data Parallelism**: Each data-parallel group processes a different mini-batch.

- **Tensor Parallelism**: Each transformer layer is split across GPUs within each group.

- **Pipeline Parallelism**: Different pipeline stages hold different groups of layers.

- **Expert Parallelism**: MoE experts are further split across GPUs.

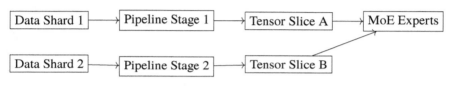

Figure 5.2: Hybrid Parallelism Workflow

Communication Optimization with NCCL

Hybrid parallelism imposes extreme communication demands. Each training step requires:

- Synchronizing gradients across data-parallel replicas.

- Transferring activations and gradients across tensor-parallel GPUs.

- Forwarding micro-batches across pipeline stages.

- Routing tokens between expert-parallel shards.

DeepSeek uses **NVIDIA Collective Communication Library (NCCL)**, heavily tuned for:

- Message size (matching network MTU).

- Overlapping communication with computation.

- Optimized collectives (AllReduce, AllGather, Scatter).

Pipeline Management with DualPipe

DeepSeek -R1s papers mention **DualPipe**, their custom pipeline engine. Though full details are unpublished, its purpose is clear:

114

- Coordinate hybrid parallelism across thousands of GPUs.

- Optimize pipeline scheduling to reduce idle bubbles.

- Overlap communication and computation to maximize throughput.

While DualPipe itself is proprietary, its principles can be emulated using open frameworks like Megatron-LM or DeepSpeed.

Distributed Training Best Practices

Readers aiming to replicate DeepSeeks setup should adopt several best practices:

- Choose shard counts divisible by total GPUs to simplify scheduling.

- Use consistent global seeds for reproducibility across distributed runs.

- Log detailed profiling data (communication time, compute time, idle time) to detect bottlenecks.

- Regularly checkpoint global states to recover gracefully from node failures.

Distributed training infrastructure is the hidden backbone of DeepSeeks success. Training 671 billion parameters across thousands of GPUs requires a carefully orchestrated dance of data parallelism, tensor parallelism, pipeline segmentation, and dynamic expert routing. By understanding and correctly combining these techniques, expert readers can construct their own scalable infrastructure to train DeepSeek-scale models reliably and efficiently.

5.4 Mixed Precision and Memory Optimization

Training DeepSeek-R1, a model with 671 billion parameters and a 128K token context window, requires not only vast computational power but also careful attention to memory efficiency. Without specialized techniques to reduce memory footprint, such a model would be infeasible to train even on the most advanced hardware. This section explores how DeepSeek-R1 achieves this through mixed precision training and complementary memory optimization techniques, ensuring that the model fits across thousands of GPUs while maintaining numerical stability and computational speed.

The Importance of Mixed Precision in Large-Scale Training

Traditional deep learning relied heavily on full precision (FP32) arithmetic, where each number uses 32 bits for storage and computation. While numerically stable, FP32 quickly becomes impractical as models scale beyond tens of billions of parameters. For models like DeepSeek-R1, the memory consumed by model weights, activations, gradients, and optimizer states would vastly exceed the limits of modern GPUs if stored in FP32. Moreover, FP32 computations are slower on modern hardware compared to lower precision formats optimized for tensor cores.

Mixed precision training addresses this by using lower-precision formats like FP16, BF16, or FP8 for the bulk of computations, while selectively retaining FP32 precision where necessary. This technique can:

- Halve or quarter memory requirements for model weights and activations.

- Improve training throughput by exploiting hardware optimized for low precision.

- Enable larger batch sizes, improving training stability.

Precision Formats and Trade-offs

The following table summarizes the primary precision formats used in large-scale training:

Format	Bits per Number	Range	Precision
FP32	32	Full	Full
BF16	16	Same exponent range as FP32	Reduced precision
FP16	16	Narrower range	Lower precision
FP8	8	Very narrow	Lowest precision

Table 5.2: Comparison of precision formats

DeepSeek -R1 notably employs FP8 for weights and activations, a more aggressive choice than the FP16 or BF16 used in earlier large models like GPT-3 or PaLM. FP8s tiny memory footprint makes it highly attractive for enormous models, but it demands careful handling to avoid severe numerical instability.

The Mixed Precision Training Process

In practice, mixed precision training operates at three levels:

116

1. **Model Weights and Forward Pass:** Stored and computed in lower precision (FP8/FP16/BF16).

2. **Gradients:** Accumulated in higher precision (often FP16 or BF16) to maintain sufficient numerical stability.

3. **Loss and Optimizer State:** Maintained in full FP32 precision to ensure small updates are not lost due to rounding.

This can be illustrated in the training loop:

```
with autocast(device_type="cuda", dtype=torch.float8_e4m3):
    output = model(input)
    loss = loss_fn(output, target)

scaler.scale(loss).backward() # Apply dynamic loss scaling
scaler.step(optimizer)
scaler.update()
```

This example shows PyTorchs autocast and GradScaler in action, though DeepSeeks real pipeline (likely implemented with custom DualPipe logic) is more complex.

FP8: Challenges and Adaptations

FP8 provides extreme memory savings, but its limited precision and range make it difficult to apply directly to all components. DeepSeek-R1 likely adopts:

- Per-tensor dynamic scaling to adapt numerical ranges on the fly.

- Higher precision for certain sensitive computations (softmax, layer normalization).

- Gradual transition to lower precision during early warmup epochs.

Per-tensor scaling, for example, applies:

$$\tilde{W} = \frac{W}{\text{scale}}$$

where scale is dynamically chosen to fit the tensor into FP8s limited range.

Memory Savings from Mixed Precision

The impact of mixed precision on memory is dramatic, as shown below:

117

Data Type	FP32 Memory (GB)	FP8 Memory (GB)
Model Weights	2,600	650
Gradients	2,600	650
Optimizer States	5,200	1,300

Table 5.3: Memory footprint for DeepSeek-R1 at different precisions

The 4x savings from FP8 is essential for fitting the model across 10,000 GPUs while maintaining workable batch sizes and context lengths.

Gradient Checkpointing

Even with mixed precision, memory remains a bottleneck when training on long sequences. In standard backpropagation, activations from every layer are retained in memory to compute gradients. This becomes impractical for DeepSeek-R1s 128K token context.

Gradient checkpointing reduces memory consumption by saving only a fraction of activations and recomputing the rest during backpropagation. This trades some compute for dramatic memory savings.

$$\frac{\partial L}{\partial x} = \frac{\partial L}{\partial y}\frac{\partial y}{\partial x}$$

Instead of storing y, the forward pass for $y = f(x)$ is repeated during backpropagation.

```
from torch.utils.checkpoint import checkpoint
output = checkpoint(layer, input)
```

Activation Packing and Offloading

For exceptionally long sequences, DeepSeek may further apply:

- Packing multiple shorter documents into a single sequence to reduce padding overhead.

- Offloading activations to CPU memory during training, though this is slower than keeping them on GPU.

Activation offloading looks like:

```
activations = activations.cpu()
```

118

This technique is typically a last resort when dealing with extreme context lengths like 128K tokens.

Combining Techniques: An Integrated Pipeline

DeepSeek -R1s final memory management stack likely resembles:

- Weights stored in FP8.

- Gradients accumulated in BF16.

- Loss and optimizer states maintained in FP32.

- Activations checkpointed every few layers.

- Activations optionally offloaded for very long sequences.

- Per-tensor dynamic scaling for FP8 tensors.

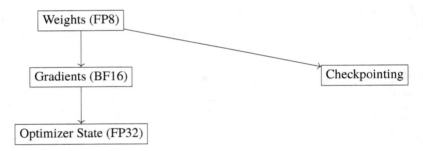

Figure 5.3: DeepSeek -R1 Memory and Precision Strategy

Performance Impact of Mixed Precision

Beyond memory savings, mixed precision also accelerates training by enabling tensor core operations:

- FP8 tensor core matmuls are up to 4x faster than FP32.

- This acceleration compounds across thousands of GPUs.

This dual benefitfaster training and smaller memory footprintis why mixed precision is essential for DeepSeek-R1.

119

Training a 671 billion-parameter model with 128K context length is impossible without aggressive precision and memory optimization. Mixed precision training using FP8, combined with gradient checkpointing and optional activation offloading, allows DeepSeek-R1 to fit within available hardware while maintaining reasonable batch sizes and training speeds. Mastering this delicate balance is essential for anyone seeking to replicate DeepSeeks infrastructure, making mixed precision one of the cornerstones of modern large-scale language model training.

5.5 Optimization Algorithms and Learning Schedule

The success of training DeepSeek-R1, a large language model with 671 billion parameters, depends critically on the choice of optimization algorithm and the design of an appropriate learning rate schedule. These decisions influence not only the speed of convergence but also the final performance and stability of the model. With extreme-scale models, poor optimization choices can lead to catastrophic divergence, slow training, or suboptimal generalization. This section explains the optimizer selection, learning rate strategies, and regularization techniques used in training DeepSeek-R1, providing expert readers with the tools needed to design robust optimization pipelines for models of similar scale.

Why Optimization Matters at Scale

Large-scale models amplify optimization challenges in several ways:

- Each training step involves billions of weight updates, so small numerical errors accumulate rapidly.

- Diverse training data (text, code, math) introduces domain shifts, making fixed learning rates unreliable.

- Sparse Mixture-of-Experts (MoE) adds further instabilityonly a small subset of experts are updated per token, introducing uneven gradient flow.

- Large batch sizes (necessary for distributed training efficiency) reduce per-step gradient variance, changing the dynamics of optimization.

For these reasons, DeepSeek-R1 requires a combination of adaptive optimization, careful regularization, and dynamic learning rate adjustment.

AdamW: The Optimizer of Choice

DeepSeek -R1 uses the AdamW optimizer, which has become the standard for large-scale transformer training. AdamW combines the adaptive learning rates of Adam with explicit weight decay regularization, striking a balance between fast convergence and weight norm control.

The AdamW update equations are:

$$m_t = \beta_1 m_{t-1} + (1 - \beta_1)g_t$$

$$v_t = \beta_2 v_{t-1} + (1 - \beta_2)g_t^2$$

$$\hat{m}_t = \frac{m_t}{1 - \beta_1^t}, \quad \hat{v}_t = \frac{v_t}{1 - \beta_2^t}$$

$$\theta_{t+1} = \theta_t - \eta \frac{\hat{m}_t}{\sqrt{\hat{v}_t} + \epsilon} - \eta \lambda \theta_t$$

where:

- g_t is the gradient at step t.

- m_t and v_t are first and second moment estimates.

- η is the learning rate.

- λ is the weight decay coefficient.

Learning Rate Warmup and Cosine Decay

Large models are notoriously sensitive to learning rates. Starting with a large learning rate risks destabilizing early layers before useful feature representations have formed. Therefore, DeepSeek-R1 applies a learning rate schedule composed of:

1. **Linear Warmup**: Gradual increase from near-zero to peak learning rate.

2. **Cosine Decay**: Smooth reduction after warmup to very small final rates.

The learning rate at step t during warmup (total warmup steps T_w) is:

$$\eta_t = \frac{t}{T_w} \cdot \eta_{max}$$

After warmup, the learning rate follows a cosine schedule over T total steps:

$$\eta_t = \eta_{min} + \frac{1}{2}(\eta_{max} - \eta_{min})\left(1 + \cos\left(\frac{t - T_w}{T - T_w}\pi\right)\right)$$

This smooth decay encourages stable convergence during late training.

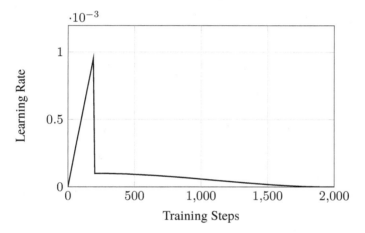

Figure 5.4: Example warmup and cosine decay schedule

Regularization Techniques

Even with proper learning rates, large models require regularization to prevent overfitting and instability. DeepSeek-R1 employs:

- **Weight Decay**: Built into AdamW, controlling parameter growth.

- **Gradient Clipping**: Applied during gradient aggregation to prevent outlier gradients from destabilizing updates:

$$g \leftarrow \frac{g}{\max\left(1, \frac{\|g\|}{\text{clip threshold}}\right)}$$

122

- **Embedding Dropout**: Small random dropout applied to input embeddings, helpful when the corpus mixes diverse domains (natural text, code, math).

ZeRO: Optimizer State Partitioning

Storing optimizer states (first and second moment estimates for AdamW) for a 671 billion-parameter model is infeasible without specialized techniques. DeepSeek-R1 likely employs the **ZeRO Optimizer**, which splits these states across GPUs. For example:

```
GPU 0: [Params 0-25%]
GPU 1: [Params 25-50%]
GPU 2: [Params 50-75%]
GPU 3: [Params 75-100%]
```

Each GPU only updates its own portion, reducing memory pressure.

Layer-wise Learning Rate Scaling

DeepSeek -R1's depth (64 layers) also motivates adjusting learning rates across layers. Upper layers typically receive smaller updates than lower layers:

$$\eta_l = \frac{\eta_0}{\sqrt{l}}$$

This scaling prevents higher layers from diverging while the lower layers converge faster.

Dynamic Loss Scaling

Since DeepSeek-R1 uses mixed precision (covered in Section 5.4), gradients can suffer underflow at low precision. Dynamic loss scaling combats this:

- Initially scale the loss by a large factor (e.g., 2^{15}).

- If gradients overflow, lower the scale.

- If gradients remain stable, gradually raise the scale.

```
loss = scaler.scale(loss)
loss.backward()
scaler.step(optimizer)
scaler.update()
```

Checkpointing and Recovery

123

DeepSeek -R1s training spans weeks, so failures are inevitable. Checkpoints include:

- Model weights.

- Optimizer state (including moments and learning rate).

- Loss scale.

- Random seeds (for deterministic resumption).

Monitoring and Diagnosis

Every training step logs:

```
Step 194800 | LR 1.3e-4 | Loss 2.91 | GradNorm 0.42 | LossScale 2048
```

This allows:

- Detecting divergence.

- Identifying learning rate schedule mistakes.

- Monitoring gradient explosion (grad norm) and precision issues (loss scale).

DeepSeek -R1s optimization strategy integrates:

- AdamW optimizer with ZeRO state partitioning.

- Learning rate warmup followed by cosine decay.

- Regularization via weight decay, gradient clipping, and embedding dropout.

- Layer-wise learning rate adjustments for deep transformers.

- Dynamic loss scaling to stabilize mixed precision.

This careful orchestration ensures the model converges reliably across trillions of tokens, delivering both efficiency and robustness.

Effective optimization is not a secondary concern in large-scale trainingit is a first-class engineering and scientific challenge. For expert readers seeking

124

to replicate DeepSeek-R1, this section offers a comprehensive blueprint covering every stage of the optimization lifecycle, from initial learning rate tuning to loss scaling and distributed optimizer partitioning. Mastering these techniques is essential to successful training at the frontier of language model scale.

5.6 Loss Computation and Tracking

In the development and training of large language models such as DeepSeek-R1, the loss function serves not only as a fundamental mathematical objective but also as a critical diagnostic signal for model health, training stability, and optimization effectiveness. Loss computation is tightly integrated into every forward and backward pass of the training pipeline, and its continuous tracking forms the backbone of both real-time monitoring and post-training analysis. This section delves into the theoretical foundation, practical implementation, and operational significance of loss computation and tracking for DeepSeek-R1s large-scale pre-training process.

Loss Function in Causal Language Modeling

DeepSeek -R1s pre-training objective is based on the widely used causal language modeling (CLM) task, which requires the model to predict the next token given all previous tokens in a sequence. Mathematically, this is framed as a conditional probability:

$$p_\theta(x_t \mid x_1, x_2, \ldots, x_{t-1})$$

The training loss is the negative log-likelihood over the training corpus, averaged across all tokens:

$$\mathcal{L} = -\frac{1}{N} \sum_{t=1}^{N} \log p_\theta(x_t \mid x_1, x_2, \ldots, x_{t-1})$$

This formulation directly reflects the language modeling task, rewarding models that assign high probability to the correct next token and penalizing incorrect predictions. The loss is computed per batch, with each GPU in a distributed setup computing its own local loss.

Token Masking and Special Handling

While the loss objective applies to most tokens equally, some tokens may be masked from loss calculation for specific reasons:

- Padding tokens added to align sequences within a batch.

- Special control tokens (e.g., document separators, metadata markers).

- Formatting tags such as <think> used to annotate reasoning traces.

In these cases, the loss for these tokens is effectively ignored:

$$\mathcal{L} = -\frac{1}{N_{\text{unmasked}}} \sum_{t=1}^{N} \mathbf{1}(x_t \notin M) \log p_\theta(x_t \mid x_{<t})$$

where M is the set of masked tokens.

Distributed Loss Aggregation

Training DeepSeek-R1 spans thousands of GPUs, each processing a distinct data shard. Each GPU computes its local batch loss, which is then aggregated across all GPUs to compute a global average loss:

$$\mathcal{L}_{\text{global}} = \frac{1}{K} \sum_{k=1}^{K} \mathcal{L}_k$$

This aggregation relies on synchronized collective communication (usually via NCCL) to ensure all nodes contribute equally to the global loss. The global loss is logged centrally for training progress tracking.

Impact of Mixed Precision on Loss Computation

As discussed in Section 5.4, DeepSeek-R1 trains using mixed precision, where forward activations, gradients, and optimizer states use lower precision (FP8, BF16). However, the loss itself is often computed in full FP32 precision to preserve numerical accuracy:

$$\mathcal{L} = -\frac{1}{N} \sum_{t=1}^{N} \log p_\theta(x_t \mid x_{<t})$$

Dynamic loss scaling (DLS) is applied to maintain stable gradients:

$$\tilde{\mathcal{L}} = S \cdot \mathcal{L}$$

where S is the dynamic scale factor adjusted based on detected under-flows/overflows in gradients.

126

Per-Domain Loss Tracking

Because DeepSeek-R1s corpus mixes diverse data sourcesnatural language, code, math problems, and reasoning datathe training pipeline tracks separate losses for each domain. This allows for domain-specific diagnostics:

$$\mathcal{L} = \sum_{d \in D} \lambda_d \mathcal{L}_d$$

where D denotes the set of domains and λ_d controls the contribution of each domain to the total loss. This enables analysis like:

Domain	Initial Loss	Current Loss
General Text	4.7	2.6
Code	5.5	3.0
Math	6.0	3.5

Table 5.4: Domain-specific loss tracking during training

Real-time Loss Monitoring and Visualization

The global loss and domain-specific losses are logged at each training step:

```
Step 142800 | Loss 2.857 | Math Loss 3.55 | Code Loss 2.98 | LR 1.24e-4
```

These logs feed into a real-time visualization dashboard, which displays:

- Current loss (global and per domain).

- Smoothed loss curve over time.

- Learning rate curve.

- Gradient norms (for detecting divergence).

This combination provides a live diagnostic window for monitoring model health.

127

Figure 5.5: Example training loss curve

Loss Spikes and Anomaly Detection

Abrupt increases in loss indicate severe training pathologies:

- Batch contamination (evaluation data leaking into training set).

- Gradient explosion due to numerical instability.

- Distributed synchronization failures.

The training pipeline automatically triggers alerts if the loss jumps unexpectedly by more than a set threshold (e.g., 20% in one step).

Evaluation Loss Tracking

Periodic evaluation on held-out validation data provides a complementary signal:

$$\mathcal{L}_{\text{eval}} = -\frac{1}{N_{\text{eval}}} \sum_{t=1}^{N_{\text{eval}}} \log p_\theta(x_t \mid x_{<t})$$

Unlike training loss, evaluation loss:

- Uses fixed data (never sampled during training).

- Tracks generalization, rather than memorization.

128

If the gap between training and evaluation loss widens too much, overfitting is suspected.

Post-training Loss Analysis

After training, complete loss logs are analyzed for retrospective insights:

- Did certain domains converge faster than others?

- Were there loss spikes linked to infrastructure events (e.g., hardware failure)?

- Were learning rate transitions (e.g., after warmup) correlated with noticeable loss changes?

These insights directly inform hyperparameter tuning for future model versions.

Loss computation and tracking is far more than just a number printed at each training step. For DeepSeek-R1, it is a core diagnostic instrument that reflects the health of optimization, the balance across training domains, the quality of data, and the numerical stability of the distributed training pipeline. Expert readers replicating DeepSeek-R1 should treat loss tracking as an integral component of the training pipeline, not a secondary reporting feature. Effective monitoring of loss curves, domain-specific losses, and periodic evaluation metrics is essential to diagnosing and correcting potential problems before they cascade into full-scale training failure.

5.7 Periodic Evaluation During Training

Periodic evaluation during the training of large language models such as DeepSeek-R1 is a fundamental component of any rigorous training pipeline. While training loss provides immediate feedback on how well the model is fitting the training data, it is insufficient for understanding generalization the models ability to handle unseen data and demonstrate robust reasoning across diverse domains. This section details how DeepSeek-R1 performs regular evaluation runs, how evaluation data is selected, which metrics are tracked, and how evaluation results feed back into model tuning, early stopping decisions, and quality assurance processes.

Purpose and Role of Periodic Evaluation

During training, models continuously optimize their parameters to minimize a training loss function, often computed on batches sampled directly from the training corpus. However, this training loss reflects how well the model memorizes or fits the training distribution, not how well it generalizes. Periodic evaluation addresses this gap by testing the model on a fixed **evaluation set** not used for training.

Periodic evaluation serves multiple purposes:

- **Detecting overfitting**: By comparing training loss to evaluation loss, researchers can assess whether the model is learning general patterns or merely memorizing.

- **Monitoring domain-specific skills**: DeepSeek-R1 is trained across text, code, and mathematics; periodic evaluation tracks how performance evolves in each domain.

- **Diagnosing data contamination**: If evaluation loss suddenly drops suspiciously, it may indicate accidental contamination between training and evaluation data.

- **Guiding early stopping**: If evaluation loss plateaus while training loss continues to improve, it may signal diminishing returns, justifying early stopping.

Evaluation Frequency and Scheduling

DeepSeek -R1s training spans trillions of tokens and multiple weeks, so evaluation is scheduled periodically rather than continuously. Typical practices include:

- Running evaluation every N steps, where N might range from 5,000 to 50,000 depending on training speed.

- Running evaluation whenever the learning rate schedule undergoes a significant shift (end of warmup, midway decay, etc.).

- Performing comprehensive evaluation after significant architectural changes, such as swapping expert routing strategies in the Mixture-of-Experts framework.

130

By maintaining a **regular cadence**, the training team can maintain up-to-date visibility into the evolving generalization capabilities of the model.

Design of the Evaluation Set

The quality and balance of the evaluation set are critical to meaningful evaluation. DeepSeek-R1s evaluation set reflects the diverse domains represented in pre-training:

- General language (news articles, encyclopedias, web pages)

- Programming problems (code completion, function generation)

- Mathematical reasoning problems (word problems, competition-style logic problems)

Domain	Proportion in Training	Proportion in Evaluation
General Text	50%	50%
Code	25%	25%
Math	25%	25%

Table 5.5: Domain balance between training and evaluation sets

To ensure robustness, DeepSeeks evaluation set is carefully curated to avoid overlap with the training data. This requires thorough deduplication, using techniques such as:

- Exact deduplication (byte-for-byte matches).

- Near deduplication (document clustering based on high overlap in token sequences).

Evaluation Metrics

The primary metric for periodic evaluation is the same cross-entropy loss used during training, applied to the held-out evaluation set:

$$\mathcal{L}_{\text{eval}} = -\frac{1}{N} \sum_{t=1}^{N} \log p_\theta (x_t \mid x_{<t})$$

However, DeepSeek also tracks domain-specific metrics:

131

- **For code**: Pass@k the proportion of programming problems solved correctly within the models top-k generated solutions.

- **For math**: Stepwise accuracy the proportion of intermediate reasoning steps that match gold-standard solutions.

- **For general text**: Perplexity the exponential of the average negative log-likelihood across all tokens.

Distributed Evaluation Process

Periodic evaluation in DeepSeek-R1 does not pause training. Instead, evaluation runs on a dedicated evaluation cluster, reading model checkpoints from shared storage. This asynchronous process ensures training throughput is unaffected while maintaining regular performance monitoring.

The process is illustrated in Figure 5.6.

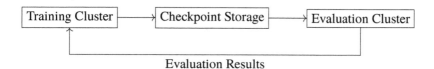

Evaluation Results

Figure 5.6: Asynchronous evaluation pipeline

Tracking Training vs. Evaluation Loss

A crucial goal of periodic evaluation is to track the **gap between training and evaluation loss**. This gap reveals:

- **Healthy learning**: Both losses decrease in parallel.

- **Overfitting**: Training loss decreases much faster than evaluation loss.

- **Data contamination**: Evaluation loss drops suspiciously (suggesting accidental overlap with training data).

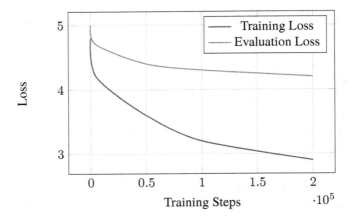

Figure 5.7: Example training vs evaluation loss

Periodic Performance Reports

After each evaluation run, a structured report is generated, summarizing:

- Current training step.

- Overall evaluation loss.

- Domain-specific metrics (pass@k for code, math accuracy, etc.).

- Trends relative to previous checkpoints.

Example:

```
Step: 320000
Eval Loss: 3.62
Pass@1 (code): 0.55
Pass@5 (code): 0.73
Math Accuracy: 82.1%
```

Role in Early Stopping Decisions

Periodic evaluation results feed directly into the decision process for **early stopping**. If evaluation loss flattens and domain-specific metrics show diminishing returns, further training may waste computational resources. Conversely, if a significant domain gap remains (e.g., code underperforms relative to text), curriculum adjustments may be made instead.

133

Periodic evaluation transforms training from a blind optimization loop into a guided, evidence-based process. By separating training loss (fit) from evaluation loss (generalization), DeepSeek-R1 ensures its reasoning capabilities emerge not just as artifacts of the training data but as true general cognitive abilities. Expert readers replicating DeepSeek-R1s training pipeline should view periodic evaluation not as an optional add-on but as an essential mechanism for quality control, scientific analysis, and responsible scaling.

Chapter 6

Evaluation and Benchmarking

This chapter explains how model performance is evaluated across all key stages, from pre-training to final reasoning assessment. It introduces the essential metrics for tracking fluency, reasoning quality, and code generation accuracy, along with the benchmark suite used for systematic testing. The chapter also covers how performance is validated through public leaderboards and reasoning-specific tests, ensuring reliable comparisons with both earlier versions and external models.

6.1 Core Evaluation Metrics

Evaluation metrics play a central role in the development, training, and benchmarking of large language models. These metrics serve as quantitative signals that guide decisions throughout the entire lifecycle of a modelfrom early pre-training diagnostics to final performance comparisons with external systems. In large-scale language model development, there is no single metric that can fully capture performance across all dimensions, so a multi-metric evaluation strategy is essential. This section introduces the core evaluation metrics used to assess fluency, reasoning capability, and code generation accuracy. Together, these metrics offer a comprehensive view of how well the model performs both linguistically and logically, as well as its ability to produce reliable outputs in task-specific contexts such as programming.

Perplexity: The Core Fluency Metric

Perplexity is the most fundamental metric for evaluating language model quality during pre-training. It measures how well a model predicts the next token given the preceding tokens. The formal definition of perplexity for a dataset of N tokens is:

$$\text{Perplexity} = \exp\left(-\frac{1}{N}\sum_{t=1}^{N}\log p_\theta(x_t \mid x_1, x_2, \ldots, x_{t-1})\right)$$

This expression computes the average log-probability assigned by the model to the correct tokens, then exponentiates the negative average to produce a measure in the range $[1, \infty)$, where lower is better.

Why Perplexity Matters

Perplexity captures the models ability to represent the statistical structure of natural language. A low perplexity indicates that the model can predict likely tokens with high confidence, while high perplexity signals uncertainty or confusion. In early training stages, perplexity often drops steeply as the model learns basic language patterns (e.g., syntax and word order). In later stages, the rate of improvement slows as the model focuses on more subtle patterns like discourse coherence, factual knowledge, and complex reasoning.

Perplexity Trends During Training

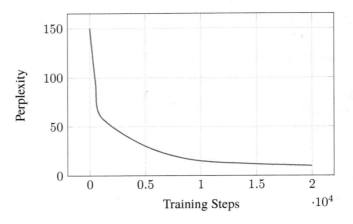

Figure 6.1: Typical perplexity curve during pre-training

A steadily decreasing perplexity confirms the model is learning, but extremely low perplexity may indicate overfittingespecially if evaluation perplexity stalls or worsens.

Pass@k: Functional Accuracy for Code Generation

Perplexity is insufficient to evaluate performance on structured tasks such as code generation. For code, correctness is binary: a program either solves a problem or it does not. The standard metric for this type of evaluation is *pass@k*, which measures how often at least one of the models top-k generated solutions is correct.

Formal Definition

Given a set of programming problems, the model generates k independent solutions for each. Pass@k is the fraction of problems for which at least one of the solutions is correct:

$$\text{pass@k} = \frac{\text{\# problems solved by at least one solution}}{\text{total problems}}$$

Example Calculation

If the model is evaluated on 100 coding problems, generating 5 solutions per problem, and 72 problems are solved correctly by at least one solution, the

137

pass@5 score is:

$$\frac{72}{100} = 0.72$$

Metric	Score
pass@1	0.53
pass@5	0.72
pass@10	0.81

Table 6.1: Example pass@k scores on code generation benchmark

Why Pass@k is Important

Pass@k recognizes that in creative domains like programming, there are many possible correct solutions. A model should not be penalized if its first output is imperfect, provided it can generate a correct answer within k tries. This reflects realistic coding scenarios, where developers refine and retry code before achieving correctness.

Stepwise Reasoning Accuracy

For reasoning tasks (e.g., mathematical problem solving), correctness is more than just getting the final answer right. What matters is the entire *reasoning process*. This is especially true for complex multi-step problems where intermediate logic must be correct for the final answer to make sense. Deep reasoning evaluation tracks:

- Correctness of intermediate steps.

- Logical coherence between steps.

- Consistency when solving similar problems with different phrasing.

Example (GSM8K Problem)

John has 12 apples. He gives 4 apples to his friend and buys 7 more. How many apples does John have now?

A reasoning-capable model should produce:

```
Step 1: Start with 12 apples.
Step 2: Subtract 4 apples given away.
Step 3: Add 7 apples bought.
Step 4: Final count = 12 - 4 + 7 = 15 apples.
```

138

Each step can be evaluated for logical correctness, and the whole process receives a stepwise accuracy score.

Reasoning-Specific Tags

To enhance reasoning transparency, models can be trained to output structured reasoning traces using special tags, e.g.,

$$\langle\texttt{think}\rangle\text{reasoning step}\langle/\texttt{think}\rangle$$

This makes it easier to evaluate not just final answers but the thinking process itself.

Benchmark-Derived Composite Scores

In addition to atomic metrics like perplexity or pass@k, evaluation often aggregates performance across entire standardized benchmark suites. For example:

Benchmark	Score
GSM8K (math)	87%
HumanEval (code)	72%
TriviaQA (knowledge)	78%

Table 6.2: Example benchmark results

These scores are useful for communicating progress to non-technical audiences, but they should not replace fine-grained metric tracking during training.

Why a Multi-Metric Approach is Essential

No single metric can capture the full competence of a large language model:

- Perplexity measures fluency but ignores correctness.

- Pass@k measures correctness but ignores fluency.

- Stepwise accuracy captures reasoning but not general linguistic quality.

To fully understand a models capabilities and limitations, researchers must track:

$$\{\text{Perplexity}, \text{Pass@k}, \text{Stepwise Accuracy}, \text{Benchmark Scores}\}$$

139

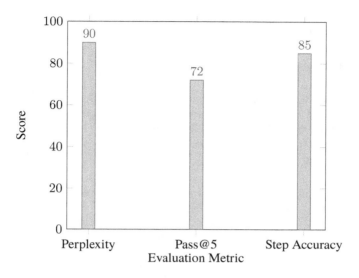

Figure 6.2: Comparison across different metrics

This section introduced the core evaluation metrics essential for understanding model progress and ensuring reliable performance across domains. Expert readers should integrate these metrics into their own training pipelines, continuously tracking not only language fluency but also functional correctness and stepwise reasoning. Only by maintaining a diverse evaluation strategy can large language models achieve balanced competence, ensuring robustness in both linguistic and logical tasks.

6.2 Benchmark Suite

The evaluation of large language models relies heavily on benchmark suitespredefined sets of tasks designed to probe specific capabilities, from language fluency to multi-step reasoning, programming proficiency, and factual knowledge retrieval. While core metrics such as perplexity provide valuable insights into the statistical quality of a models predictions, benchmarks enable a more holistic and domain-specific evaluation. This section details the benchmark suite used to evaluate the models described in this book, explaining the rationale behind each selection, the skills it measures, and the pre-processing required to ensure reproducibility in evaluation.

The Purpose of Benchmark Evaluation

Benchmarks serve as standard reference points that allow models to be compared not only to their predecessors, but also to other publicly available models. Well-constructed benchmarks focus on real-world tasks that are representative of how users interact with language models. In practice, a benchmark suite serves multiple purposes:

- Providing a stable, external point of comparison across development cycles.

- Capturing task-specific performance beyond general fluency.

- Highlighting domain strengths and weaknesses (e.g., mathematical reasoning versus code generation).

- Ensuring that evaluation remains stable over time, avoiding metric drift from changing internal test sets.

Mathematical Reasoning Benchmarks

Mathematical reasoning is a key area of focus for modern models, especially those designed for reasoning-centric applications. The benchmark suite includes:

GSM8K A benchmark consisting of grade-school math word problems. Each problem requires several simple reasoning steps, such as arithmetic calculations, to arrive at the correct answer. Models are expected to break problems into steps, reason about intermediate results, and compute final answers.

MATH500 A more advanced benchmark, consisting of competition-level math problems drawn from sources such as the American Mathematics Competitions. These problems require abstract thinking, multi-step reasoning, and symbolic manipulation.

AIME Problems sourced from the American Invitational Mathematics Examination (AIME). These are designed to challenge the upper limits of high school mathematical ability, requiring both creative insight and rigorous logic.

Benchmark	Difficulty	Steps Required	Example Task
FP32	Medium	510	Solve basic algebraic equations.
BF16	Low	15	Simple arithmetic tasks.
FP16	Medium	510	Evaluate polynomial expressions.
INT8	High	>10	Complex geometry problems.

Table 6.3: Mathematical benchmarks in the suite

Code Generation Benchmarks

The ability to generate, complete, or repair code is another critical capability for modern models. The benchmark suite includes:

HumanEval A widely-used benchmark for function completion, where models are given natural language docstrings and asked to generate correct implementations in Python.

MBPP (Mostly Basic Python Programming) A benchmark focused on simpler programming tasks, ideal for evaluating fundamental code generation skills such as loop construction, string processing, and arithmetic.

Codeforces-like problems A custom set of programming challenges drawn from competitive programming contests. These problems are more algorithmic, requiring logical thinking, recursion, and dynamic programming.

Benchmark	Difficulty	Steps Required	Example Task
HumanEval	Medium	25	Complete a function given a description.
MBPP	Easy	13	Write short Python functions from descriptions.
Codeforces	High	>5	Solve competitive programming problems.

Table 6.4: Programming benchmarks in the suite

142

General Knowledge and Open-Domain QA Benchmarks

General knowledge is a core dimension of language model competence. The benchmark suite includes:

TriviaQA   A large-scale question answering benchmark focused on factoid questions spanning history, science, culture, and more. Answers tend to be single facts.

NaturalQuestions   This benchmark reflects real user queries submitted to search engines, capturing ambiguities, multi-step reasoning, and factual lookup in realistic contexts.

OpenBookQA   A science knowledge benchmark that requires reasoning with a small open book of science facts, combining knowledge retrieval with logical deduction.

Benchmark	Question Source	Knowledge Domain
TriviaQA	Curated Trivia	General Knowledge
NaturalQuestions	Search Logs	Open-Domain
OpenBookQA	Science Facts	Science

Table 6.5: General knowledge benchmarks in the suite

Pre-processing and Formatting

Before evaluation, each benchmark undergoes several pre-processing steps to ensure consistency with the models training tokenizer and input format:

- Tokenization using the same tokenizer applied during training.

- Removal of extraneous formatting, if present (e.g., HTML tags, markdown artifacts).

- Standardization into a clear prompt-response format, especially for multi-step reasoning problems where intermediate steps should be explicitly shown.

For example, a GSM8K question might be formatted as:

```
Question: John has 12 apples. He gives 4 apples to his friend and buys 7 more
.
How many apples does John have now?

<think>
Step 1: Start with 12 apples.
Step 2: Subtract 4 apples given away.
Step 3: Add 7 apples bought.
Step 4: Final count = 12 - 4 + 7 = 15 apples.
</think>

Answer: 15
```

Multi-domain Evaluation and Composite Scoring

Because large models are expected to handle diverse tasks, evaluation does not focus solely on one benchmark. Instead, scores across different domains are aggregated into a composite score. A balanced formula might be:

$$\text{Composite Score} = 0.4 \times \text{Math Score} + 0.4 \times \text{Code Score} + 0.2 \times \text{QA Score}$$

This ensures no single domain can dominate the final assessment.

Avoiding Contamination and Data Leakage

For reproducibility, the evaluation suite must be completely disjoint from training data. This is verified by:

- Deduplication removing any benchmark data found in the pre-training corpus.

- URL matching removing web pages directly linked to evaluation examples.

- Metadata screening removing content labeled as derived from evaluation datasets.

This ensures models are not unfairly advantaged by memorization.

A well-constructed benchmark suite acts as the ultimate proving ground for large language models. It moves beyond raw statistical fit to measure practical performance across key domains such as math, programming, and knowledge retrieval. To faithfully replicate the evaluation process described in this book, expert readers must adopt these benchmarks, apply consistent pre-processing, and track composite scores over time. These practices ensure not only fairness and transparency, but also meaningful comparison between models trained at different scales or under different data and architecture choices.

6.3 Leaderboard Comparison and External Validation

The development of large language models requires more than just internal evaluation on curated test sets. To establish a models true performance and ensure its credibility within the broader research community, external validation through public leaderboards and direct comparisons with state-of-the-art models is essential. External benchmarking offers a common ground, where models trained by different teams under varying conditions are tested under the same protocols, using identical datasets and metrics. This ensures transparency, reproducibility, and fair assessment of progress. This section explains the purpose, methodology, and best practices for external validation, with a focus on how language model developers position their work on global leaderboards.

Why External Validation Matters. While internal test sets provide valuable diagnostic feedback during training, they are inherently limited by the data selection process, potential biases, and differences in task design between different research teams. External validation addresses these limitations in several ways:

- **Standardized Test Sets**: Public leaderboards use pre-defined, widely agreed-upon test sets, ensuring all models are evaluated on identical data.

- **Cross-Team Comparability**: Results from different teams are presented side-by-side, enabling direct comparisons under consistent conditions.

- **Transparency and Reproducibility**: External benchmarks allow third parties to re-run the same tests, ensuring published results are verifiable.

Without external benchmarking, model performance claims lack credibility, particularly in highly competitive domains like reasoning and code generation.

Selection of Public Leaderboards. Several leaderboards have become authoritative reference points for evaluating language models. For LLMs, the following are most relevant:

Open LLM Leaderboard: The Open LLM Leaderboard tracks the performance of publicly available models across tasks including general language understanding, reasoning, math, and code generation. It is particularly useful for open-source models aiming to establish their standing against both proprietary systems and peer open-source projects.

HELM (Holistic Evaluation of Language Models): HELM provides a structured framework for evaluating models across a broader set of dimensions, including robustness, fairness, and bias, in addition to core reasoning and generation capabilities. This broader focus ensures that performance claims account for potential ethical and safety concerns.

BigCode Leaderboard: Specifically designed for evaluating code generation models, BigCodes leaderboard tracks performance on widely used programming benchmarks such as HumanEval and MBPP. For models trained to generate or complete code, this leaderboard provides the most relevant external validation.

Leaderboard	Primary Focus	Common Benchmarks Used
Open LLM	General LLMs	GSM8K, MMLU, HumanEval
HELM	Holistic Capabilities	TriviaQA, SQuAD, TruthfulQA
BigCode	Code Generation	HumanEval, MBPP

Table 6.6: Relevant leaderboards for external LLM validation

External Comparison Metrics. The metrics used for external comparison largely overlap with internal evaluation metrics, but they are applied within stricter protocols to ensure fair comparisons. The most important metrics include:

GSM8K Accuracy: GSM8K (Grade School Math 8K) measures the proportion of math problems the model solves correctly, with a focus on stepwise reasoning. This metric captures logical reasoning rather than just language fluency.

Pass@k: Pass@k is used for code generation, measuring how often the model

146

produces a correct solution within its top-k attempts. Both HumanEval and MBPP rely heavily on pass@k.

MMLU (Massive Multitask Language Understanding): MMLU aggregates performance across 57 distinct subjects, including history, law, biology, and mathematics. It serves as a proxy for broad domain knowledge and reasoning capabilities.

Perplexity (Optional in External Validation): Although perplexity is crucial internally, it is less emphasized in public leaderboards, as it measures fluency rather than task-specific competence. Nonetheless, some evaluations (especially language modeling challenges) may report perplexity for completeness.

Models Used for Comparison. To make external validation meaningful, models must be compared against relevant baselines. The key comparative groups are:

1. **Proprietary Leaders** — GPT-4, Claude, Gemini, which set upper bounds for performance.

2. **Leading Open-Source Models** — LLaMA 2, Mistral, StarCoder, representing the best of what can be achieved under open-source conditions.

3. **Earlier Generations** — Previous versions of the same model, to document internal progress.

Model	Type	Availability
GPT-4	Proprietary	Closed-source
LLaMA 2	Open-source	Public weights
Mistral	Open-source	Public weights
StarCoder	Open-source (Code focus)	Public weights

Table 6.7: Model baselines for external comparison

Ensuring Fair Comparisons. For external validation to be credible, strict procedures must be followed:

- All models must be evaluated on the **same test sets**.

- Identical **prompt templates** should be used across models.

147

- Sampling strategies (temperature, top-p, etc.) must be **standardized**.

- Any post-processing (e.g., normalizing answers for math problems) should be applied equally to all models.

For example, a typical evaluation pipeline for GSM8K might look like:

```
# Standard prompt
Q: John has 12 apples. He gives 4 to his friend and buys 7 more. How many apples
    does John have now?
A:

# Model inference (with identical sampling across all models)
output = model.generate(prompt, temperature=0.7, top_p=0.95)

# Post-processing
extracted_answer = extract_final_number(output)
```

Reporting External Validation Results. Transparency is essential when publishing external validation results. Best practices include:

- Clear disclosure of **pre-training data sources** (especially if overlaps with benchmarks exist).

- Explicit documentation of **training compute budget** and model size.

- Clear separation of results obtained via **zero-shot prompting** versus those involving fine-tuning on related data.

An ideal leaderboard submission might resemble:

```
Model: MyLLM-65B
Pre-training Data: 3T tokens (filtered Common Crawl, books, math, code)
Compute: 2.5 million GPU hours (A100-80GB)
Prompting Method: Standard GSM8K prompt (no task-specific tuning)
GSM8K Accuracy: 85.2%
```

Why External Validation Benefits the Broader Community. External validation benefits not only the models developers but also the broader research and user communities:

- Builds **trust** in published results.

- Encourages **fair competition** by forcing all participants to play by the same rules.

148

- Provides downstream users (researchers, developers) with reliable data to select the best models for their needs.

- Allows the entire field to **track progress** over time through consistent historical comparisons.

No large language model can claim to be state-of-the-art without robust external validation. Public leaderboards, applied under consistent and transparent evaluation conditions, are the only reliable way to benchmark progress against both historical models and current competitors. Experts seeking to replicate the processes described in this book should prioritize external benchmarking not merely as a reporting requirement, but as an essential scientific practice that reinforces credibility, transparency, and continuous progress in large-scale AI research.

6.4   Specialized Reasoning Tests

Evaluation of large language models has evolved significantly over the past several years, driven by the growing realization that pure fluency and factual recall metrics are insufficient to capture deeper reasoning capabilities. While language models have become increasingly capable of generating fluent and factually correct text, true reasoning abilityunderstanding, planning, and logically deriving solutions to complex problemsremains a much harder challenge. This section explores the specialized reasoning tests used to assess these abilities, focusing on mathematical reasoning, stepwise logic, and structured multistep problem solving. These tests form a critical component of the evaluation process for models designed to excel at analytical thinking, problem decomposition, and structured inference.

Why Reasoning Evaluation is Distinct.

Reasoning is fundamentally different from tasks like language modeling or factual recall. Language modeling metrics such as perplexity measure a models ability to predict the next token in fluent text, while factual QA benchmarks assess the retrieval and regurgitation of specific knowledge. In contrast, reasoning evaluation focuses on the process by which the model derives conclusions. This includes:

- Breaking down complex problems into solvable steps.

149

- Maintaining logical consistency across steps.

- Detecting and correcting errors mid-process.

- Producing verifiable chains of reasoning, rather than just final answers.

These requirements call for specialized benchmarks that explicitly test reasoning steps—not just outcomes—and demand evaluation procedures capable of capturing intermediate reasoning quality.

Benchmarks for Evaluating Reasoning.

To measure reasoning performance effectively, the evaluation suite must include benchmarks explicitly designed for multi-step logic and mathematical reasoning. Three core benchmarks serve this purpose:

GSM8K. This dataset consists of grade-school math word problems, typically solvable within 2 to 4 reasoning steps. It captures fundamental arithmetic reasoning, making it a useful probe for baseline reasoning ability. Problems resemble:

> John has 12 apples. He gives 4 apples to his friend and buys 7 more. How many apples does John have now?

MATH500. This more advanced benchmark contains problems from math competitions, often requiring abstract algebra, geometry, and combinatorial reasoning. Solutions can span up to 10 reasoning steps and frequently involve symbolic manipulation.

AIME. Sourced from the American Invitational Mathematics Examination, this benchmark presents some of the most challenging problems. These require creative insight, multi-step reasoning, and often a combination of algebraic transformation, logical deduction, and case analysis.

Benchmark	Average Steps	Difficulty Level
GSM8K	2–4 steps	Easy
MATH500	5–10 steps	Intermediate
AIME	10+ steps	Advanced

Table 6.8: Summary of mathematical reasoning benchmarks

Structured Reasoning Output.

Unlike factual QA, where a single word or phrase answer suffices, reasoning problems require complete reasoning chains. To enable reliable evaluation, models are often required to produce structured reasoning outputs, for example:

```
<think>
Step 1: John starts with 12 apples.
Step 2: John gives away 4 apples.
Step 3: John buys 7 more apples.
Step 4: Total = 12 - 4 + 7 = 15 apples.
</think>
Answer: 15
```

This format allows evaluators to check the process, not just the answer, enabling partial credit if some steps are correct even if the final result is wrong.

Stepwise Accuracy as a Core Metric.

In reasoning evaluation, a models accuracy can be decomposed into:

- **Final Answer Correctness**: Whether the last answer is correct.

- **Stepwise Accuracy**: Proportion of intermediate reasoning steps that match ground-truth solutions.

Stepwise accuracy offers diagnostic insight—allowing researchers to pinpoint whether failures stem from early misunderstanding, mid-process arithmetic errors, or final step misjudgments.

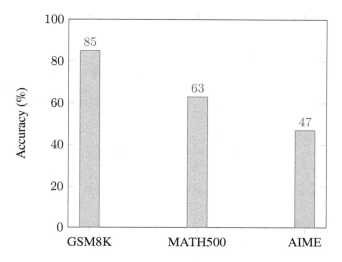

Figure 6.3: Stepwise reasoning accuracy across benchmarks

Process Supervision and Reasoning Alignment.

Reasoning-focused models are increasingly trained with *process supervision*, where training data explicitly includes stepwise reasoning traces rather than just final answers. This improves:

- Logical coherence across steps.

- Adherence to correct reasoning formats.

- Error detection, by allowing the model to spot inconsistencies as it generates.

Example training instance:

```
Q: Alice sells 3 boxes of apples with 10 apples each. How many apples did she sell
    ?
A:
<think>
Step 1: Each box contains 10 apples.
Step 2: There are 3 boxes.
Step 3: Total apples = 3 * 10 = 30 apples.
</think>
A: 30
```

152

This explicit trace teaches the model to always explain itself.

Reflection and Self-Verification.

Another innovation in reasoning evaluation is the use of reflection prompts. After producing an initial reasoning chain, the model is asked to review its own work and identify potential mistakes. This self-verification step helps:

- Catch arithmetic slip-ups.

- Identify skipped logical steps.

- Reinforce careful checking as a core skill.

Example reflection prompt:

```
Please review the following reasoning. Highlight any logical, arithmetic, or
factual errors:
<think>
Step 1: ...
Step 2: ...
...
</think>
```

Combining Process and Answer Evaluation.

The final evaluation combines:

$$\text{Total Reasoning Score} = 0.6 \times \text{Final Answer Correctness} + 0.4 \times \text{Stepwise Accuracy}$$

This formula rewards both getting the right answer and reasoning correctly to reach it.

Benchmark	Final Answer Accuracy	Stepwise Accuracy
GSM8K	85%	90%
MATH500	63%	72%
AIME	47%	60%

Table 6.9: Combined reasoning performance across benchmarks

Reasoning Trends Across Training Stages.

Reasoning ability does not emerge uniformly during training. Early stages optimize fluency and factual recall, while reasoning often improves more sharply

153

during late-stage fine-tuning, particularly when specialized math, logic, and code datasets are introduced.

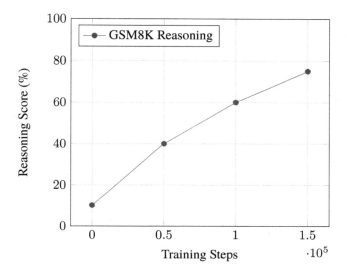

Figure 6.4: Reasoning score over training stages

Specialized reasoning tests provide a far richer and more meaningful signal than traditional fluency metrics when evaluating models intended for analytical tasks. By tracking stepwise accuracy, training models to produce structured reasoning traces, and incorporating reflection-based review, researchers can ensure that models develop not only factual knowledge, but also the reasoning skills necessary to apply that knowledge correctly.

Chapter 7

DeepSeek Training Infrastructure and Essential Tools

DeepSeek has developed a robust, scalable infrastructure that enables the training of some of the world's largest AI models. This chapter delves into the essential tools that form the backbone of DeepSeek's training pipeline. By integrating specialized components for expert-parallel communication, bidirectional pipeline parallelism, distributed data access, and optimized attention computations, DeepSeek achieves unprecedented levels of speed, scalability, and efficiency. In the sections that follow, we explore these tools—DeepEP, DualPipe, 3FS, and FlashMLA—in detail, illustrating their roles and integration within a PyTorch-based training workflow. This discussion aims to provide both the technical insights and practical guidance necessary for researchers and engineers to harness the full potential of large-scale AI model training.

7.1 DeepEP: Expert-Parallel Communication Library

DeepEP is a custom communication library tailored for Mixture-of-Experts (MoE) models, where specialized sub-networksknown as expertsare spread across multiple GPUs or nodes. In these architectures, a gating network assigns each input token to one or more experts for parallel processing. This distribution, however, demands efficient, all-to-all communication: tokens must be quickly sent to the appropriate experts and their outputs gathered back seamlessly. DeepEP addresses this challenge by providing optimized, high-throughput GPU kernels that manage both the dispatch and the combination of tokens with minimal latency.

Key Features and Practical Benefits

- **Optimized Dispatch and Combine Kernels:**
  DeepEP implements dedicated CUDA kernels that handle two critical operations:

  - *Dispatch:* Routes input tokens to the designated experts across GPUs.
  - *Combine:* Collects and reassembles the processed outputs from the experts into the original token order.

  These operations are optimized for both intra-node transfers (using NVLink) and inter-node transfers (leveraging RDMA), ensuring that communication overhead remains very low even in large-scale setups.

- **Low-Precision Data Transfer:**
  DeepEP supports low-precision data formats such as FP8 and BF16. This capability reduces the volume of data transferred between devices without compromising model accuracy, thereby increasing the effective throughput of the system.

- **Overlapping Communication with Computation:**
  By using asynchronous data transfers and managing dependencies through CUDA events, DeepEP allows communication to occur simultaneously with local computation. This overlap means that while tokens

156

are being sent or received, the GPU can continue with other computations, maximizing hardware utilization.

- **Inference Optimization:**
  For applications like autoregressive generation where tokens are processed one-by-one, DeepEP offers low-latency RDMA kernels. These optimizations reduce the delay in streaming tokens between experts, leading to faster response times in production environments.

A Practical Workflow for Integrating DeepEP in a PyTorch MoE Pipeline

To illustrate the practical integration of DeepEP, consider the following step-by-step workflow that shows how to embed it into a PyTorch-based training loop:

1. Distributed Setup   Before leveraging DeepEP, initialize the distributed environment so that each GPU (or process) is aware of its role. For example:

```
import torch.distributed as dist
dist.init_process_group(backend='nccl', init_method='env://')
world_size = dist.get_world_size()
rank = dist.get_rank()
```

In this setup, each GPU is responsible for processing a subset of the experts.

2. Token Routing and Dispatch   After the gating network assigns tokens to experts (for example, using a top-k selection), use DeepEP to compute a dispatch layout. This layout determines how many tokens need to be sent to each expert and to which GPU. The following code snippet shows how to initialize DeepEPs buffer and perform the dispatch:

```
from deep_ep import Buffer, EventOverlap
_buffer = Buffer() % Initialize the global buffer

# Assume topk_idx contains the expert assignment for each token,
# and total_number_of_experts is defined.
(num_toks_per_rank, num_toks_per_rdma_rank, num_toks_per_expert,
 is_token_in_rank, prev_event) = _buffer.get_dispatch_layout(topk_idx,
        total_number_of_experts, async_finish=True)

recv_x, recv_idx, recv_weights, tokens_per_expert, handle, event = _buffer.
        dispatch(
```

```
x, topk_idx=topk_idx, topk_weights=topk_weights,
num_tokens_per_rank=num_toks_per_rank,
num_tokens_per_rdma_rank=num_toks_per_rdma_rank,
is_token_in_rank=is_token_in_rank,
num_tokens_per_expert=num_toks_per_expert,
async_finish=True, allocate_on_comm_stream=True)
```

Here, the dispatch call is non-blocking so that while tokens are being sent to their target experts, the GPU can begin processing other tasks.

3. Expert Computation and Result Combination Once each GPU receives its designated tokens, the expert modules perform their forward computation. After processing, DeepEPs combine function gathers these outputs and reorders them to match the original token sequence:

```
expert_outputs = []
for expert_id, num_tokens in enumerate(tokens_per_expert):
    if num_tokens == 0:
        continue % Skip experts that did not receive any tokens
    expert_input = recv_x[recv_idx == expert_id]
    expert_output = expert_layers[expert_id](expert_input)
    expert_outputs.append(expert_output)
local_outputs = torch.cat(expert_outputs, dim=0)

combined_x, _, event = _buffer.combine(local_outputs, handle, async_finish=True,
    previous_event=event)
```

The combine operation ensures that every tokens output is placed back in its original order, ready for the next stage of the network.

4. Backward Pass Integration DeepEP also provides routines for the backward pass, such as dispatch_backward and combine_backward. These functions manage the reverse flow of gradients across GPUs so that end-to-end training can proceed without manual intervention.

Practical Tips

- **Leverage Asynchronicity:** Use the asynchronous options provided by DeepEP to overlap data transfers with computation. This will help in reducing idle time on the GPUs.

- **Monitor Token Distribution:** Ensure that your gating network distributes tokens evenly among experts to avoid bottlenecks where some experts are overloaded while others remain idle.

- **Test on a Small Scale First:** Before deploying on a large multi-GPU setup, validate your integration with a small-scale test. This helps catch configuration issues early and ensures that the communication patterns work as expected.

By abstracting the low-level details of inter-GPU communication, DeepEP enables researchers and engineers to focus on developing robust MoE models, confident that the underlying communication overhead is efficiently managed.

7.2 DualPipe: Bidirectional Pipeline Parallelism

Large-scale models often exceed the memory capacity of a single GPU, so their layers must be distributed across multiple devices using pipeline parallelism. Traditional pipeline parallelism, however, tends to suffer from idle "bubbles" where GPUs wait during either the forward or backward pass. DualPipe overcomes these inefficiencies by interleaving forward and backward computations in a bidirectional manner, ensuring that every stage in the pipeline remains actively engaged.

Core Concepts and Advantages

- **Overlapping Forward and Backward Passes:**
  DualPipe injects micro-batches at both ends of the pipeline. This enables one stage to process the forward pass of one micro-batch while another stage simultaneously computes the backward pass of a different micro-batch. Such interleaving minimizes idle time and maximizes hardware utilization.

- **Parameter Duplication for Concurrent Processing:**
  To facilitate simultaneous forward and backward computations within the same stage, DualPipe duplicates model parameters. While this approach increases memory usage, it allows each stage to operate on separate parameter copies concurrently, significantly boosting throughput.

- **Enhanced Communication-Compute Overlap:**
  DualPipe leverages asynchronous data transfers and non-blocking communication (using primitives like `torch.distributed.send` and `recv`) alongside multiple CUDA streams. This design effectively

159

hides the latency of data transfers, ensuring that communication does not stall computation.

Integrating DualPipe in a PyTorch Distributed Environment

Implementing DualPipe involves partitioning the model into stages, splitting the training batch into multiple micro-batches, and then scheduling these micro-batches so that forward and backward passes overlap. Below is a simplified example for a single pipeline stage:

```
fwd_queue = list(micro_batches) # Micro-batches awaiting forward pass
bwd_queue = [] # Micro-batches awaiting backward pass
outputs = [None] * len(micro_batches)
gradients = [None] * len(micro_batches)

time_step = 0
while fwd_queue or bwd_queue:
    # Launch forward pass if a micro-batch is available
    if fwd_queue:
        mb = fwd_queue.pop(0)
        out = stages_fwd[0](mb) # Execute forward pass on stage 0
        send_to_next_stage(out, stage=0) # Non-blocking send to the next stage
        bwd_queue.append(mb) # Schedule micro-batch for backward pass

    # Launch backward pass if gradients are available from the next stage
    if gradients_available_from_next_stage(stage=0):
        grad_input = recv_grad_from_next_stage(stage=0)
        grad_out = stages_bwd[0].backward(grad_input) # Execute backward pass on
            stage 0
        accumulate_gradients(grad_out, mb) % Accumulate gradients for parameter
            updates

    time_step += 1
```

In a full multi-stage pipeline, each stage follows similar logic with careful coordination of non-blocking communications and parallel CUDA streams. DeepSeeks open-source DualPipe library provides a complete reference implementation along with profiling tools, allowing fine-tuning of the schedule to achieve near 100% GPU utilizationeven when combining Mixture-of-Experts with pipeline parallelism.

Practical Considerations

- **Even Partitioning:**
  Ensure that your model is split evenly into stages and that the micro-

160

batches are balanced. This symmetry is crucial for effective bidirectional scheduling.

- **Memory Management:**
  While parameter duplication increases memory requirements, the resulting throughput gains generally outweigh the cost. If memory is a constraint, consider complementary techniques such as gradient checkpointing.

- **Monitoring and Profiling:**
  Use the profiling tools provided in the DualPipe library to monitor pipeline performance. Fine-tuning the scheduling can help identify and eliminate bottlenecks, ensuring smooth overlap between computation and communication.

By interleaving forward and backward passes and overlapping communication with computation, DualPipe significantly reduces idle time in the training pipeline. This leads to more efficient use of GPU resources and accelerates the training of extremely large models.

7.3   3FS: Distributed File System for AI Training Data

For large-scale AI training, fast and reliable access to massive datasets is as crucial as efficient model computation. 3FS (Fire-Flyer File System) is DeepSeeks distributed file system that delivers rapid, high-throughput data access across thousands of GPUs. By integrating high-speed NVMe SSDs with RDMA-capable networks, 3FS creates a unified storage solution that scales effortlessly with increasing data and compute demands.

Architectural Highlights and Practical Benefits

- **Disaggregated Storage and Scalability:**
  3FS aggregates storage from multiple nodes, each equipped with high-speed NVMe SSDs, to achieve an overall read throughput that scales with the number of nodes. Data is striped and replicated across servers, ensuring that even the most demanding training workloads can access data at speeds comparable to local disk access.

- **RDMA-Optimized Data Transfers:**
  By leveraging RDMA (Remote Direct Memory Access), 3FS minimizes CPU involvement and reduces latency during data transfers. This
  is especially beneficial when handling large checkpoint files or streaming high volumes of training data.

- **Strong Consistency and POSIX Compliance:**
  Utilizing chain replication and a stateless metadata service, 3FS guarantees strong consistency across all operations. Its full POSIX-compliant
  interface means that standard data-loading tools, such as PyTorchs Dat-
  aLoader, work seamlessly without any modifications.

- **Optimized for Diverse Data Workloads:**
  Whether dealing with millions of small files or large multi-gigabyte
  datasets, 3FS is engineered for efficient random access, global shuffling,
  and parallel writes. This versatility makes it an ideal solution for both
  streaming training data and managing checkpoint storage.

Integrating 3FS with PyTorch

Integrating 3FS into your training workflow is straightforward, especially
when it is mounted as a standard file system (e.g., at /mnt/3fs). For example,
using an ImageFolder dataset for ImageNet:

```
import torchvision.datasets as dsets
import torchvision.transforms as T
from torch.utils.data import DataLoader
from torch.utils.data.distributed import DistributedSampler

data_root = "/mnt/3fs/data/imagenet"
train_set = dsets.ImageFolder(root=f"{data_root}/train", transform=T.ToTensor())

# For distributed training, use a DistributedSampler to ensure each process reads a
        unique subset.
sampler = DistributedSampler(train_set, num_replicas=world_size, rank=rank,
        shuffle=True)
train_loader = DataLoader(train_set, batch_size=256, sampler=sampler, num_workers
        =8)
```

In this setup, each training node directly accesses data from 3FS over the network. The inherent caching and block-aligned read operations further boost
performance, ensuring that GPUs are continuously fed with data without requiring local copies or pre-sharded datasets.

162

Practical Considerations

- **Mounting and Configuration:**
  Ensure that 3FS is correctly mounted on all training nodes (e.g., /mnt/3fs). Tuning configuration options like cache size and block alignment based on workload and network conditions can further optimize performance.

- **Data Organization:**
  Organize datasets into a hierarchical directory structure to reduce directory listing overhead and enhance file access performance.

- **Monitoring Throughput:**
  Utilize system tools (e.g., iostat) or dedicated 3FS monitoring utilities to track I/O throughput and ensure that the file system meets your training demands.

- **Distributed Sampling:**
  When using distributed training, always employ a DistributedSampler to ensure each process accesses a unique subset of data, minimizing redundant transfers and maximizing efficiency.

By integrating 3FS into your training pipeline, you eliminate common data access bottlenecks, allowing your GPU clusters to focus on processing and learning from vast datasets.

7.4 FlashMLA: Efficient Attention Kernel Optimization

Transformer models rely on attention mechanisms to capture complex relationships in data. However, traditional attention computations require forming large matrices that scale quadratically with sequence length, which can quickly become a memory and speed bottleneck. FlashMLA is DeepSeeks specialized attention kernel designed to address these challenges by optimizing both speed and memory usage through advanced techniques such as tiling, fusion, and latent compression.

Innovations and Practical Benefits

- **Tiled and Fused Computations:**
  FlashMLA breaks the attention computation into smaller, manageable tiles rather than materializing the entire attention matrix. This tiling approach reduces memory consumption and enhances cache locality, leading to faster execution.

- **Low-Rank Key-Value Compression:**
  By compressing the key-value (KV) cache to roughly 6.7% of its original size, FlashMLA allows transformers to support much longer sequences without suffering from quadratic memory growth. This latent attention mechanism shares information across heads or employs low-dimensional projections, resulting in an approximate 15 reduction in KV storage.

- **Paged KV Cache and Precision Optimization:**
  The kernel organizes keys and values into fixed-size pages, streamlining memory access and handling variable-length sequences efficiently. Leveraging NVIDIA Hopper GPUs' advanced tensor cores with BF16/FP16 precision, FlashMLA achieves near-peak performanceup to 580 TFLOPS on H800 GPUswhile maintaining numerical stability.

Integrating FlashMLA into Transformer Models

Integrating FlashMLA into your transformer model involves replacing the standard multi-head attention module with one that calls the FlashMLA kernel. The following steps offer a practical guide for using FlashMLA with PyTorch.

1. Installation and Import Ensure FlashMLA is installed in your environment, and import the necessary functions:

```
from flash_mla import get_mla_metadata, flash_mla_with_kvcache
```

2. Custom Attention Module Below is a simplified implementation of an attention module that uses FlashMLA:

```
import torch
import torch.nn as nn
```

```
class FlashMLAAttention(nn.Module):
    def __init__(self, embed_dim, num_heads):
        super().__init__()
        self.num_heads = num_heads
        self.head_dim = embed_dim // num_heads
        self.W_q = nn.Linear(embed_dim, embed_dim)
        self.W_k = nn.Linear(embed_dim, embed_dim)
        self.W_v = nn.Linear(embed_dim, embed_dim)
        self.W_o = nn.Linear(embed_dim, embed_dim)

    def forward(self, x, key_cache=None, cache_seqlens=None):
        batch, seq_len, _ = x.size()
        # Compute query, key, and value projections
        Q = self.W_q(x).view(batch, seq_len, self.num_heads, self.head_dim)
        K = self.W_k(x).view(batch, seq_len, self.num_heads, self.head_dim)
        V = self.W_v(x).view(batch, seq_len, self.num_heads, self.head_dim)

        # For training, use current K and V as the cache
        if key_cache is None:
            key_cache = K
            val_cache = V
            cache_seqlens = torch.IntTensor([seq_len] * batch).to(x.device)
        else:
            # For inference, append new projections to the existing cache
            key_cache = torch.cat([key_cache, K], dim=1)
            val_cache = torch.cat([V], dim=1)
            cache_seqlens += 1

        # Generate tiling metadata based on cache sequence lengths
        tile_meta, num_splits = get_mla_metadata(cache_seqlens, s_q=self.num_heads,
              h_kv=self.num_heads)

        # Execute the FlashMLA kernel with causal masking enabled
        output, lse = flash_mla_with_kvcache(Q, key_cache, None, cache_seqlens,
                                  self.head_dim, tile_meta, num_splits, causal
                                  =True)
        # Reshape and project the output back to the original embedding dimension
        out = output.reshape(batch, seq_len, -1)
        return self.W_o(out), key_cache, val_cache, cache_seqlens
```

3. Usage in a Model The custom attention module can now be integrated into your transformer model. For example:

```
attn = FlashMLAAttention(embed_dim=1024, num_heads=16).cuda()
x = torch.randn(32, 128, 1024, device='cuda') # Example input: batch of 32,
      sequence length 128
out, key_cache, val_cache, cache_seqlens = attn(x)
loss = some_loss_function(out)
loss.backward() # Gradients propagate through the FlashMLA kernel seamlessly
```

By reducing the memory footprint and accelerating the attention computation, FlashMLA enables transformer models to handle longer sequences and larger batch sizes. This optimization is pivotal for both training and inference, making FlashMLA a key component in DeepSeeks approach to scaling state-of-the-art transformer models.

DeepSeek 's training infrastructure combines specialized tools that address key challenges in scaling AI models. DeepEP optimizes MoE communication, DualPipe eliminates pipeline idle time through bidirectional scheduling, 3FS delivers high-throughput distributed data access, and FlashMLA accelerates attention mechanisms while reducing memory overhead. Together, these components form an integrated ecosystem that pushes the boundaries of large-scale model training, allowing researchers and engineers to focus on innovation rather than infrastructure bottlenecks.

Chapter 8

DeepSeek Model Architecture and Optimization Techniques

DeepSeek 's large language models achieve state-of-the-art performance through a carefully designed architecture combined with advanced optimization techniques. This chapter covers the essential architectural features of DeepSeek's models, including the use of Mixture-of-Experts (MoE) layers, position encoding innovations, and attention scaling. It also highlights optimization techniques applied during training, including expert parallelism, efficient attention, and custom data pipelines. Together, these design and optimization strategies enable DeepSeek models to scale efficiently across thousands of GPUs while maintaining competitive accuracy and throughput.

8.1 Mixture-of-Experts (MoE) in DeepSeek Models

DeepSeek models leverage a sparse Mixture-of-Experts (MoE) architecture to dramatically scale model capacity without a proportional increase in computation. Instead of using a single, dense feed-forward network in every transformer block, MoE replaces it with a collection of specialized expert sub-networks. For each input token, only a small subset of these experts is activated, enabling massive overall capacity while keeping the per-token computation manageable.

For example, DeepSeek-V3 contains a total of 671 billion parameters; however, due to sparse activation, only about 37 billion parameters are active per token. This design not only reduces the computational cost but also enables the model to handle a wide variety of tasks by routing tokens to experts best suited for processing them.

How MoE Works in DeepSeek Models

In an MoE layer, the standard feed-forward network is replaced by multiple expert sub-networks. A gating network first examines the hidden representation of each token and produces a score for every expert. By applying a softmax function over these scores, the gating network converts them into probabilities. DeepSeek commonly employs *top-k gating* (with $k = 2$), meaning that for each token, only the two experts with the highest probabilities are selected. The output of the MoE layer is then computed as a weighted sum of the outputs from these selected experts:

$$y = \sum_{i \in \text{Top-}k(h)} G_i(h)\, E_i(h),$$

where h is the input hidden state, $E_i(h)$ is the output of the i-th expert, and $G_i(h)$ is the corresponding gating weight. This approach allows the model to scale up its capacityby adding more expertswithout increasing the compute per token linearly.

Expert Specialization and Load Balancing

A major advantage of the MoE architecture is that it promotes expert specialization. Over the course of training, different experts tend to learn to handle specific types of patterns or tasks. For instance, one expert might focus on syntactic structures, while another might specialize in factual recall. The gating network dynamically routes tokens to the most relevant experts, effectively ensembling many specialized sub-models.

However, ensuring a balanced distribution of tokens across experts is crucial. If a few experts are overused while others are underutilized, it can lead to training instability and inefficient use of model capacity. DeepSeek addresses this issue by incorporating a load balancing loss into the training objective. This auxiliary loss encourages the gating probabilities to be evenly distributed among experts. One common method is to penalize the variance in expert utilization, for example by computing the coefficient of variation:

$$CV^2 = \frac{\text{Var}(I)}{(\text{Mean}(I))^2},$$

where $I_i = \sum_{\text{tokens}} G_i(h)$ represents the total gating weight for expert i. Minimizing this term helps ensure that each expert receives a roughly equal share of the tokens. In newer versions like DeepSeek-V3, a refined group-limited gating mechanism is used to naturally maintain a balanced load without the need for an explicit auxiliary loss.

A Practical Implementation Example

Below is a simplified PyTorch-like pseudocode that demonstrates the implementation of a sparse MoE layer with top-k gating (with $k = 2$):

```
import torch
import torch.nn.functional as F

class MOELayer(torch.nn.Module):
    def __init__(self, d_model, num_experts, k=2):
        super().__init__()
        self.k = k
        self.num_experts = num_experts
        # Gating network: produces a score for each expert
        self.gate = torch.nn.Linear(d_model, num_experts)
        # Expert networks: each expert is an independent feed-forward network
        self.experts = torch.nn.ModuleList([ExpertFFN(d_model) for _ in range(
            num_experts)])

    def forward(self, x):
        # x shape: (batch, seq_len, d_model)
        batch_size, seq_len, d_model = x.shape
        # Compute gating logits for each token
        logits = self.gate(x) # shape: (batch, seq_len, num_experts)
        # Select top-k experts for each token
        topk_vals, topk_idx = torch.topk(logits, self.k, dim=-1) # shape: (batch,
            seq_len, k)
        # Create a mask that zeros out non-topk experts
        mask = torch.full_like(logits, float('-inf'))
        mask.scatter_(dim=-1, index=topk_idx, src=topk_vals)
        # Apply softmax to get gating probabilities (only top-k get non-zero values)
```

```
gates = F.softmax(mask, dim=-1) # shape: (batch, seq_len, num_experts)
# Initialize output tensor
output = torch.zeros(batch_size, seq_len, d_model, device=x.device)
# Dispatch tokens to experts and collect results
for expert_idx, expert in enumerate(self.experts):
    # Identify tokens for which this expert is among the top-k
    token_mask = (topk_idx == expert_idx).any(dim=-1) # shape: (batch,
        seq_len)
    if token_mask.any():
        expert_in = x[token_mask] # select tokens assigned to this expert
        expert_out = expert(expert_in) # process tokens via expert network
        # Weight expert outputs by the corresponding gating probabilities
        output[token_mask] += expert_out * gates[token_mask, expert_idx].
            unsqueeze(-1)
return output
```

In this pseudocode, the gating network computes a score for each expert, and only the top two experts are activated per token. The tokens output is the weighted sum of the selected experts outputs. In a production environment, the dispatch-and-combine operations would be optimized furtheroften using custom CUDA kernels and parallel communication across devices.

DeepSeek s use of Mixture-of-Experts allows the model to achieve massive capacity by distributing computation across hundreds of billions of parameters, while keeping the per-token computational cost nearly constant. Through efficient expert selection, dynamic routing, and load balancing, the MoE architecture enables expert specialization and robust performance across diverse tasks, making training and inference both scalable and cost-effective.

8.2 Advanced Position Encoding Strategies

Handling very long input sequences is a significant challenge for DeepSeek models, which can support context lengths up to 128K tokens. To address this, DeepSeek employs advanced position encoding strategies that not only capture relative positional information effectively but also keep computational costs manageable. This section details two key innovations: **Rotary Position Embeddings (RoPE)** and **Sliding Window Attention**, which together ensure long-range coherence without excessive computational overhead.

Rotary Position Embeddings (RoPE)

Rotary Position Embeddings (RoPE) are used to inject high-quality positional information into the transformers attention mechanism. Instead of adding fixed positional embeddings to the input, RoPE applies a position-dependent rotation to the query and key vectors in each attention head. Specifically, for each position t and each paired dimension $(2i, 2i + 1)$ in the query (or key) vector, a rotation is applied:

$$\begin{pmatrix} q_{t,2i} \\ q_{t,2i+1} \end{pmatrix} = \begin{pmatrix} \cos(\theta_t) & -\sin(\theta_t) \\ \sin(\theta_t) & \cos(\theta_t) \end{pmatrix} \begin{pmatrix} q_{t,2i}^{\text{orig}} \\ q_{t,2i+1}^{\text{orig}} \end{pmatrix},$$

where the angle θ_t is typically a monotonic function of the position t (for example, $\theta_t = t \cdot \omega$ with a base frequency ω). This rotation embeds relative positional information directly into the dot product $q_t \cdot k_s$, as differences in rotation angles between positions t and s encode their relative distance.

DeepSeek extends the standard RoPE approach by using a *decoupled* variant within its Multi-Head Latent Attention (MLA) framework. In decoupled RoPE, the positional encoding is applied in a separate latent space or to a reduced-dimensional sub-projection of the query and key vectors. This adjustment helps prevent issues that can arise with very long sequencessuch as excessive rotation angles that may degrade some dimensionsthereby ensuring that the positional encoding remains stable up to the 128K token context limit.

Below is an illustrative snippet showing how one might apply RoPE in a Py-Torch attention module:

```
def apply_rope(q, k, seq_dim=-2):
    # q, k have shape (..., seq_len, head_dim)
    seq_len = q.size(seq_dim)
    half_dim = q.size(-1) // 2 # assume head_dim is even
    pos = torch.arange(seq_len, device=q.device, dtype=torch.float)
    # Compute inverse frequencies for each pair of dimensions
    inv_freq = 10000**(-torch.arange(0, half_dim, 2, device=q.device).float()/
        half_dim)
    # Compute rotation angles: outer product of position indices and inverse
        frequencies
    angles = torch.einsum('n,d->nd', pos, inv_freq)
    # Expand angles to cover paired dimensions by repeating each angle twice
    cos = torch.cos(angles).repeat_interleave(2, dim=1)
    sin = torch.sin(angles).repeat_interleave(2, dim=1)
    # Apply rotations: combine cosine and sine components for each pair
    q_rot = q * cos.unsqueeze(0) + torch.stack([-q[...,1::2], q[...,::2]], dim=-1).
        reshape(q.shape) * sin.unsqueeze(0)
    k_rot = k * cos.unsqueeze(0) + torch.stack([-k[...,1::2], k[...,::2]], dim=-1).
        reshape(k.shape) * sin.unsqueeze(0)
    return q_rot, k_rot

# Example usage inside an attention forward pass:
q, k, v = self.Wq(x), self.Wk(x), self.Wv(x) # linear projections
q = q.view(batch, seq_len, n_heads, head_dim).transpose(1,2)
k = k.view(batch, seq_len, n_heads, head_dim).transpose(1,2)
```

```
v = v.view(batch, seq_len, n_heads, head_dim).transpose(1,2)
q, k = apply_rope(q, k, seq_dim=2)
attn_scores = torch.matmul(q, k.transpose(-1, -2)) * (1.0 / math.sqrt(head_dim))
```

In practice, DeepSeeks decoupled RoPE may apply these rotations in a latent subspace or reset the rotation periodically, ensuring robust performance over very long contexts.

Sliding Window Attention for Long Contexts

While RoPE efficiently encodes positional information, the quadratic cost of full self-attention remains a challenge when handling very long sequences. To address this, DeepSeek employs a **sliding window attention** mechanism. Instead of allowing each token to attend to all previous tokens, sliding window attention restricts the receptive field to a fixed-size window W (e.g., 2048 tokens). This means that each token attends only to tokens within the range $[t - W, t]$, drastically reducing computational requirements from quadratic to linear with respect to sequence length.

The sliding window attention works as follows:

- **Local Attention:** Each token attends to a fixed number of preceding tokens. This ensures that the most recent contextoften the most relevantis prioritized.

- **Sequential Processing:** As the sequence is processed, the attention window slides forward, ensuring continuity of context across segments.

- **Causal Constraint:** For autoregressive models, the sliding window naturally incorporates causality by preventing tokens from attending to future positions.

An example implementation of a sliding window attention mask in PyTorch might look like this:

```
L = seq_len
W = window_size # e.g., 2048
mask = torch.full((L, L), float('-inf')) # initialize all positions as masked
for t in range(L):
    start = max(0, t - W)
    mask[t, start:t+1] = 0 # allow attention for tokens within the window
# Use the mask as an additive term in softmax attention
attn_weights = torch.softmax(attn_scores + mask, dim=-1)
```

This approach limits each tokens attention to a manageable number of positions, ensuring that the overall attention complexity grows linearly with sequence length (for a fixed W). Information from tokens outside the window can still be propagated through multiple layers, effectively stitching together long-range dependencies over the depth of the model.

Synergy of RoPE and Sliding Window Attention

By combining RoPE with sliding window attention, DeepSeek achieves a balance between high-quality positional encoding and computational efficiency. RoPE provides detailed relative position information within each window, while the sliding window mechanism keeps the attention computation feasible even for extremely long contexts. Together, these techniques enable DeepSeek models to process inputs as long as entire books or multi-document contexts, preserving long-range coherence without incurring prohibitive memory or time costs.

Advanced position encoding strategies in DeepSeekincluding decoupled Rotary Position Embeddings and sliding window attentionallow the model to maintain context awareness and long-range coherence efficiently. These innovations ensure that, even at context lengths up to 128K tokens, the model can operate effectively, making it well-suited for processing very long documents or conversations. The techniques are integrated into the model architecture in a way that is largely transparent to the user, allowing practitioners to simply specify longer sequences and trust that the underlying mechanisms will handle positional information robustly.

8.3 Memory-Efficient Attention Optimizations

As models grow larger and context lengths extend into the tens or hundreds of thousands of tokens, the memory and compute cost of self-attention become critical bottlenecks. DeepSeek addresses these challenges by incorporating a suite of memory-efficient attention optimizations. In particular, it leverages three complementary techniques:

1. **Flash Attention** an IO-aware algorithm that reorders attention computations into manageable tiles,

2. **Grouped-Query Attention (GQA)** a method that reduces redundant key/value storage across heads, and

3. **Low-Rank Key/Value Cache Compression** a custom technique that compresses long-term context into a compact representation.

These innovations not only reduce the memory footprint but also accelerate both training and inference, making it feasible to work with models that support 128K context and billions of parameters.

Flash Attention

Flash Attention is designed to overcome the quadratic memory requirements of standard attention. In conventional self-attention, the computation of softmax weights involves materializing a full $L \times L$ attention matrix for a sequence of length L, which is both memory intensive and slow due to repeated high-bandwidth memory (HBM) accesses. Flash Attention tackles this by:

- **Tiling the Computation:** The sequence is divided into smaller blocks that fit in the GPU's on-chip SRAM.

- **On-Chip Computation:** Within each tile, the softmax and weighted sum are computed without ever materializing the full attention matrix.

This careful reordering of operations reduces memory usage from quadratic to linear in L and significantly cuts down on data transfers between GPU memory and on-chip caches. Modern frameworks (e.g., PyTorch 2.0) expose this functionality through calls such as:

```
import torch.nn.functional as F

# q, k, v: shape (batch, heads, seq_len, head_dim)
# This call utilizes Flash Attention kernels on supported hardware.
attn_output = F.scaled_dot_product_attention(q, k, v, attn_mask=None, is_causal=
    True)
```

Empirical benchmarks show that Flash Attention can reduce memory usage by up to 10 at longer sequence lengths (e.g., 4K8K tokens) and can speed up training by keeping data on-chip.

174

Grouped-Query Attention (GQA)

Grouped-Query Attention (GQA) is an intermediate approach between standard multi-head attention and multi-query attention (MQA). In MQA, all query heads share a single key and value, drastically reducing memory requirements but potentially harming model expressiveness. GQA generalizes this idea by dividing the attention heads into G groups, where $1 \leq G \leq H$ (with H being the total number of heads). Each group uses its own key and value projections shared among a subset of query heads. This approach offers the following benefits:

- **Memory Savings:** The size of the key/value cache is reduced roughly by a factor of G. For instance, if $G = 8$ in a model with 64 attention heads, the KV cache storage is reduced by 8.

- **Quality Preservation:** Unlike full MQA (where $G = 1$), GQA preserves more diversity across heads by allowing each group to specialize.

A sketch of a GQA implementation in PyTorch might look like:

```
H = num_heads
G = kv_groups # number of key/value groups (e.g., 8)
head_dim = d_model // H

# Linear projections: Q with shape (B, L, H, head_dim); K and V with shape (B, L, G,
    head_dim)
q = Wq(x).view(B, L, H, head_dim)
k = Wk(x).view(B, L, G, head_dim)
v = Wv(x).view(B, L, G, head_dim)

# Expand keys and values to have one per head by repeating each group
expand_factor = H // G
k_expanded = k.repeat_interleave(expand_factor, dim=2) % shape: (B, L, H, head_dim
    )
v_expanded = v.repeat_interleave(expand_factor, dim=2) % shape: (B, L, H, head_dim
    )

# Proceed with standard multi-head attention using q, k_expanded, and v_expanded.
scores = torch.einsum('B L h d, B L h d -> B h L L', q, k_expanded) / math.sqrt(
    head_dim)
```

This approach reduces the memory footprint of the key/value cache while retaining most of the benefits of full multi-head attention.

Low-Rank Key/Value Cache Compression

For extremely long contexts, the key and value caches can become prohibitively large. DeepSeek introduces a custom low-rank compression technique to address this issue. The key insight is that the key K and value V matrices often contain redundant information and lie in a lower-dimensional subspace. By applying a low-rank factorization, the model can represent these matrices in a compressed form without significantly degrading the attention outputs.

In practice, learned projection matrices $P_K \in \mathbb{R}^{d_h \times r}$ and $P_V \in \mathbb{R}^{d_h \times r}$ (with $r < d_h$) are used to compress K and V:

$$K' = K \, P_K, \quad V' = V \, P_V,$$

where $K \in \mathbb{R}^{L \times d_h}$ and $V \in \mathbb{R}^{L \times d_h}$. The attention computation then proceeds in the compressed space:

$$\text{scores} = Q(K')^\top \quad \text{and} \quad \text{context} = \text{softmax}(\text{scores}) \, V',$$

followed by a reconstruction step (if needed) to map the context back to the original dimension:

$$\text{context\_full} = \text{context} \, P_V^\top.$$

A simple illustration in PyTorch pseudocode is as follows:

```
d = 128 # original head dimension
r = 64 # compressed dimension

# Learned projection matrices
P_K = torch.nn.Parameter(torch.randn(d, r))
P_V = torch.nn.Parameter(torch.randn(d, r))

# During the forward pass:
K = compute_keys(x) # shape: (batch, seq_len, d)
V = compute_values(x) # shape: (batch, seq_len, d)

# Compress K and V to lower dimensions
K_comp = K @ P_K # shape: (batch, seq_len, r)
V_comp = V @ P_V # shape: (batch, seq_len, r)

# Compute attention using compressed keys and values
scores = torch.matmul(Q, K_comp.transpose(-1, -2)) / math.sqrt(r)
attn_weights = torch.softmax(scores, dim=-1)
context_comp = torch.matmul(attn_weights, V_comp)

# Optionally, reconstruct context back to original dimension
context = context_comp @ P_V.t() # shape: (batch, seq_len, d)
```

By training the model end-to-end with these low-rank projections, DeepSeek ensures that the compressed representations retain the essential information needed for accurate attention, thereby reducing memory usage and speeding up data transfers.

Together, Flash Attention, Grouped-Query Attention, and low-rank KV cache compression form a powerful trio that makes full-attention on very long sequences feasible. Flash Attention optimizes the computation to run in on-chip memory, GQA reduces the redundancy in key/value storage across attention heads, and low-rank compression further shrinks the memory footprint of long-term context. These techniques are largely orthogonal, meaning they can be combined to achieve multiplicative improvements in efficiencyan approach that is central to DeepSeek's ability to scale to 128K token contexts while maintaining competitive training and inference speeds.

8.4 Pipeline and Expert Parallelism in DeepSeek Models

Scaling DeepSeek models to teraflop compute regimesusing hundreds or even thousands of GPUsrequires sophisticated parallelism strategies. To meet this challenge, DeepSeek employs a combination of **pipeline parallelism** and **expert parallelism** that work in concert to distribute computation effectively across devices. In recent Open-Source Week releases, the DeepSeek team introduced **DualPipe**, a bidirectional pipeline parallelism algorithm, along with **DeepEP**, an expert-parallel communication library. Together, these approaches ensure that enormous Mixture-of-Experts (MoE) models, composed of many layers and a large number of experts, can be trained efficiently across large GPU clusters.

Pipeline Parallelism (DualPipe)

Pipeline parallelism splits the neural network into sequential stages, with each stage assigned to a different device (or group of devices). During training, a large mini-batch is divided into multiple micro-batches that flow through the pipeline in a staggered fashion. In a naive pipeline, once a micro-batch completes the forward pass in one stage, that stage might remain idle while waiting for the subsequent stage to finish its computation. DualPipe overcomes this limitation by overlapping forward and backward passes.

- **Bidirectional Scheduling:** DualPipe injects micro-batches at both the beginning and the end of the pipeline. This means that while the forward pass for one micro-batch is propagating from the first to the last stage, the backward pass for a previous micro-batch can simultaneously flow from the last stage back to the first.

- **Minimized Idle Time:** Through careful scheduling and asynchronous communication, DualPipe ensures that each pipeline stage is almost always busyeither computing a forward chunk or processing a backward gradientthereby dramatically improving throughput.

For example, consider a pipeline split into 4 stages across 4 GPU nodes. With DualPipe, stage 1 might process the forward pass of micro-batch $i + 1$ while stage 2 processes the forward pass of micro-batch i and stage 3 is already handling the backward pass of micro-batch i. Although the scheduling details can be complex, frameworks like PyTorchs pipeline module or DeepSpeeds pipeline engine help automate this process. A simple two-stage example using PyTorchs experimental pipeline module might look like:

```
import torch.distributed.pipeline.sync as pipelining

# Assume the model has been split into two parts, each assigned to a different GPU.
model_stage1 = Stage1().to('cuda:0')
model_stage2 = Stage2().to('cuda:1')

# Create a pipeline module that splits the input into 8 micro-batches (chunks)
pipe = pipelining.PipelineModule(
    layers=[model_stage1, model_stage2],
    devices=['cuda:0', 'cuda:1'],
    chunks=8
)
```

DualPipe extends these ideas by further overlapping backward passes, reducing idle time and boosting hardware utilization even when the number of pipeline stages increases.

Expert Parallelism (DeepEP)

In DeepSeeks MoE architecture, only a small subset of experts is active for each token. Rather than placing all experts on a single device, **expert parallelism** distributes them across multiple GPUs. For instance, if an MoE layer contains 64 experts and 8 GPUs are available, each GPU might host 8 experts.

178

This distribution introduces an all-to-all communication pattern:

- During the forward pass, each GPU must send token representations to the GPUs hosting the corresponding experts.

- After processing, the outputs from the experts are gathered and re-ordered to match the original token order.

DeepEP is the specialized library that handles this complex communication efficiently. It provides custom GPU kernels for dispatching tokens to experts (the scatter phase) and for gathering their outputs back (the gather phase), making full use of high-speed interconnects such as NVLink (for intra-node transfers) and RDMA (for inter-node transfers). DeepEP even supports low-precision transfers (e.g., FP8) to further reduce communication overhead.

A simplified example of setting up expert parallelism in PyTorch might involve creating distributed process groups. Suppose the total world size is 64 and the expert parallel size is set to 8; then, the experts for a given MoE layer can be grouped into 8 shards, with each group handling a portion of the experts:

```
import torch.distributed as dist
world_size = dist.get_world_size()
EP_size = 8 # Number of GPUs per expert group
rank = dist.get_rank()

# Determine group index for expert parallelism
expert_group_idx = rank // EP_size
# Create a process group for the current expert parallel shard
expert_group = dist.new_group(ranks=list(range(expert_group_idx * EP_size,
                                      (expert_group_idx + 1) * EP_size)))
```

Within each expert group, an all-to-all operation (using, for example, `dist.all_to_all`) is used to shuffle token representations to the appropriate GPUs, and later to gather the processed outputs. This expert parallelism enables the model to scale the number of experts without exceeding the memory limits of individual GPUs.

Synergy of Pipeline and Expert Parallelism

By combining pipeline parallelism and expert parallelism, DeepSeek achieves multi-dimensional parallelism:

- **Pipeline Parallelism** ensures that the layers of the model are distributed

179

and that each GPU remains busy through overlapping forward and backward passes.

- **Expert Parallelism** distributes the numerous experts in MoE layers across GPUs, reducing per-device memory load and ensuring efficient all-to-all communication.

For instance, a DeepSeek-V3 training run might configure:

- 8 pipeline stages,

- 64 experts per MoE layer distributed across expert groups, and

- Additional data parallelism for handling large batches.

These strategies are orchestrated using frameworks such as DeepSpeed, FairScale, or custom libraries like DeepEP and DualPipe, which together maximize GPU utilization and enable training of models with hundreds of billions of parameters in an efficient, cost-effective manner.

In summary, DeepSeeks training infrastructure leverages advanced pipeline parallelism (DualPipe) to ensure continuous GPU utilization and expert parallelism (via DeepEP) to distribute the load of MoE layers across many devices. This multi-dimensional parallelism not only enables scaling to thousands of GPUs but also dramatically reduces training time and cost, making it possible to train massive models such as DeepSeek-V3 (with 671 billion parameters) efficiently.

8.5 Data Preprocessing and Augmentation Pipelines

Training a model as large as DeepSeek requires a highly optimized data pipeline that can efficiently feed trillions of tokens to the model. DeepSeeks data preprocessing innovations focus on two key areas: **dynamic document splitting** and **on-the-fly tokenization**. Together, these techniques ensure that the model receives long, coherent contexts and that the input pipeline never becomes a bottleneck during large-scale training.

Dynamic Document Splitting

Traditional large language model (LLM) training pipelines often use a simple concatenate and chunk approach. In this method, all documents in the corpus are concatenated into one long stream and then split into fixed-length sequences (e.g., 2048 tokens). While straightforward, this method tends to break natural document boundaries, leading to abrupt transitions and loss of context at the chunk boundaries. Such disruptions can negatively affect the models ability to capture long-range dependencies and may increase factual errors or hallucinations.

DeepSeek addresses these issues with **dynamic document splitting**, an intelligent chunking strategy that adapts to the natural structure of the text. Key aspects include:

- **Coherent Chunking:** Rather than always starting new sequences at fixed offsets, the dynamic splitter randomizes split points or uses sliding windows. This approach helps preserve the natural flow of text, ensuring that the model occasionally sees complete document endings or smooth transitions between related texts.

- **Best-Fit Packing:** When documents are shorter than the maximum sequence length, the pipeline packs multiple documents into a single sequence. This minimizes wasted space and reduces the number of arbitrary truncations. Best-fit packing algorithms approximate a solution to the bin-packing problem, ensuring that short documents are combined in a way that maintains contextual integrity.

- **Dynamic Shuffling Across Epochs:** The splitting strategy can vary slightly with each training epoch. For example, one epoch might split a long document at one point, while the next epoch uses a different split position. This variability exposes the model to multiple continuous segments from the same document, further enhancing its ability to model long-range dependencies.

A simplified pseudocode illustration for dynamic document splitting is shown below:

```
import random

max_len = 2048
sequences = []
```

181

```
for doc in documents:
    tokens = tokenizer.encode(doc) # on-the-fly tokenization is applied later
    if len(tokens) <= max_len:
        sequences.append(tokens)
    else:
        # For long documents, split into chunks with optional overlap
        start = 0
        while start < len(tokens):
            end = min(len(tokens), start + max_len)
            chunk = tokens[start:end]
            sequences.append(chunk)
            # Optionally add overlap or randomize the next starting point
            start += max_len

# Pack shorter documents together to minimize padding waste
packed_sequences = []
current_seq = []
for tokens in sequences:
    if len(current_seq) + len(tokens) <= max_len:
        current_seq.extend(tokens)
    else:
        packed_sequences.append(current_seq)
        current_seq = tokens.copy()
if current_seq:
    packed_sequences.append(current_seq)
```

This approach helps maintain *contextual integrity* by ensuring that each training sample is as contiguous as possible, enabling the model to learn long-range dependencies more effectively.

On-the-Fly Tokenization

Rather than pre-tokenizing and storing massive tokenized datasetswhich can be storage-intensive and inflexibleDeepSeek employs **on-the-fly tokenization**. Using a lightweight tokenizer built on the Rust-based HuggingFace `tokenizers` library, raw text is converted into tokens dynamically during training. This offers several advantages:

- **Storage Efficiency:** There is no need to maintain a separate, large-scale tokenized dataset, reducing storage requirements.

- **Flexibility and Dynamic Processing:** On-the-fly tokenization allows for dynamic document splitting and adaptive preprocessing, so that changes to the vocabulary or filtering criteria can be applied without reprocessing the entire corpus.

- **Parallelism and Throughput:** Tokenization can be parallelized across multiple CPU cores (or even GPUs, if needed), ensuring that the data pipeline can keep pace with the training process. This concurrent processing minimizes idle time on the GPUs.

Below is an example of how on-the-fly tokenization might be integrated into a PyTorch data pipeline using HuggingFace Datasets:

```
from datasets import load_dataset
from deepseek_tokenizer import DeepSeekTokenizer # a lightweight tokenizer
import torch

tokenizer = DeepSeekTokenizer() # instantiate the DeepSeek tokenizer
dataset = load_dataset('text', data_files={'train': 'my_corpus.txt'})['train']

def process_example(example):
    text = example['text']
    tokens = tokenizer.encode(text)
    # Apply dynamic splitting if needed
    return {'tokens': tokens}

# Tokenize each example on the fly and remove raw text column
dataset = dataset.map(process_example, remove_columns=['text'], batched=False)

def collate_fn(batch):
    # Batch is a list of dicts containing 'tokens'
    max_len = max(len(item['tokens']) for item in batch)
    # Pad sequences to the length of the longest sequence in the batch
    input_ids = [item['tokens'] + [tokenizer.pad_id] * (max_len - len(item['tokens'
        ]))
            for item in batch]
    return {'input_ids': torch.tensor(input_ids, dtype=torch.long)}

loader = torch.utils.data.DataLoader(dataset, batch_size=8, collate_fn=collate_fn)
for batch in loader:
    input_ids = batch['input_ids'].to('cuda')
    outputs = model(input_ids)
    # Training loop continues...
```

In this example, the raw text is tokenized as each example is loaded, and the resulting tokens are immediately processed by a custom collate function. This on-the-fly approach reduces preprocessing latency and keeps the data pipeline flexible and efficient.

DeepSeek s data preprocessing and augmentation pipelines are engineered for both quality and scalability. Dynamic document splitting ensures that training samples retain coherent context, while on-the-fly tokenization minimizes storage requirements and adapts dynamically to the training process. Together, these strategies enable DeepSeek models to learn from trillions of tokens efficiently and effectively, without the data pipeline becoming a performance bottleneck.

8.6 Optimization Example: Pretraining DeepSeek-R1

In this section, we present a detailed walkthrough of the pretraining work-flow for **DeepSeek -R1**, a 671B-parameter, reasoning-optimized Mixture-of-Experts (MoE) model (with roughly 37B active parameters per token). DeepSeek-R1 is trained on a diverse corpus that includes general text, mathematics, and code. In this example, we focus on the massive distributed training phase that integrates all the innovations discussed in earlier sectionsnamely, advanced MoE design, dynamic position encoding, memory-efficient attention mechanisms, multi-dimensional parallelism, and high-throughput data pipelines.

Step 1: Environment Setup and Parallel Configuration

Pretraining DeepSeek-R1 requires a large-scale distributed setup. For illustration, consider a cluster with 1024 GPUs across 128 nodes. Our training configuration uses:

- **8-way Pipeline Parallelism** (via DualPipe),

- **64-way Expert Parallelism** (via DeepEP), and

- **2-way Data Parallelism**.

Thus, the total number of processes is $8 \times 64 \times 2 = 1024$. The following pseu-docode outlines the initialization of distributed groups using PyTorch with the NCCL backend:

```
import torch
import torch.distributed as dist

dist.init_process_group(backend='nccl')
world_size = dist.get_world_size() # Should be 1024
rank = dist.get_rank()

# Define degrees of parallelism
pipeline_stages = 8
expert_parallel = 64
data_parallel = 2
assert world_size == pipeline_stages * expert_parallel * data_parallel

# Compute group indices (assuming rank ordering: pipeline, expert, then data
    parallel)
```

```
data_group_idx = rank // (pipeline_stages * expert_parallel)
pipeline_group_idx = (rank % (pipeline_stages * expert_parallel)) //
    expert_parallel
expert_group_idx = rank % expert_parallel

# Create process groups for each parallel dimension
dp_group = dist.new_group(
    ranks=[r for r in range(data_group_idx * pipeline_stages * expert_parallel,
                    (data_group_idx + 1) * pipeline_stages * expert_parallel)
                    ]
)
pp_group = dist.new_group(
    ranks=[r for r in range(data_group_idx * pipeline_stages * expert_parallel +
        expert_group_idx,
                        (data_group_idx + 1) * pipeline_stages * expert_parallel
                            + expert_group_idx,
                        expert_parallel)]
)
ep_group = dist.new_group(
    ranks=[r for r in range(data_group_idx * pipeline_stages * expert_parallel +
                    pipeline_group_idx * expert_parallel,
                    data_group_idx * pipeline_stages * expert_parallel +
                    pipeline_group_idx * expert_parallel + expert_parallel)]
)
```

In this configuration:

- **DP Group:** Contains all ranks that are replicas in data parallel.

- **PP Group:** Contains ranks corresponding to the same pipeline stage across expert shards.

- **EP Group:** Contains ranks within a pipeline stage that host different experts.

Frameworks such as DeepSpeed or Megatron-LM typically manage these groupings automatically based on a specified parallelism configuration.

Step 2: Model Initialization and Partitioning

DeepSeek -R1s architecture is built around 80 transformer layers with a hidden size of 7168. Every second layer is an MoE layer, with each MoE layer containing 64 experts. Other key model settings include:

- 64 attention heads using Grouped-Query Attention (GQA) with 8 key/-value groups,

185

- Rotary Position Embeddings (RoPE) with a decoupled configuration,

- Memory-efficient attention via FlashAttention, and

- A maximum training context of 4096 tokens (with plans to gradually extend this to longer contexts).

A simplified model configuration and initialization might be:

```
from deepseek import DeepSeekConfig, DeepSeekModel

config = DeepSeekConfig(
    num_layers=80,
    d_model=7168,
    num_heads=64,
    rope=True,
    rope_decoupled=True,
    max_position_embeddings=4096,
    moe_layers=[1, 3, 5, ..., 79],
    num_experts=64,
    expert_ffn_dim=28672, # e.g., 4x d_model
    gating_top_k=2,
    use_gqa=True,
    num_key_value_groups=8,
    use_flash_attn=True
)
model = DeepSeekModel(config)
```

Given the 8-way pipeline parallelism, the 80 transformer layers are split into 8 stages (10 layers per stage). Each process corresponding to a pipeline stage holds its assigned layers:

```
# Assume model.transformer_layers is a list of all transformer layers.
my_pipeline_idx = pipeline_group_idx # from distributed setup
my_layers = model.transformer_layers[my_pipeline_idx*10 : (my_pipeline_idx+1)*10]
model_stage = torch.nn.Sequential(*my_layers).to(device)
```

For MoE layers, expert parallelism ensures that the 64 experts are sharded across the 64 GPUs in the expert group (each GPU hosting one expert for that layer). The DeepEP library handles the all-to-all communication necessary to dispatch tokens to the appropriate experts and gather the outputs efficiently.

Step 3: Data Loading and Preprocessing

DeepSeek -R1 is pretrained on a diverse corpus, which includes text, code, and math content. The data pipeline employs dynamic document splitting and on-the-fly tokenization to generate sequences of 4096 tokens. Each process reads its own shard of the data to avoid duplication. For example, using an `IterableDataset`:

```
from torch.utils.data import DataLoader, IterableDataset

class TextDataset(IterableDataset):
    def __iter__(self):
        # Each rank reads its own data shard (e.g., based on rank)
        with open(f"data_shard_{rank}.txt", "r") as file:
            for doc in file:
                tokens = tokenizer.encode(doc.strip())
                # Split tokens into chunks of max_length (e.g., 4096)
                start = 0
                while start < len(tokens):
                    yield torch.tensor(tokens[start:start+4096], dtype=torch.long)
                    start += 4096

dataset = TextDataset()
loader = DataLoader(dataset, batch_size=1) # One sequence per iteration per worker
```

This approach ensures that raw text is tokenized and split dynamically, preserving document coherence and maximizing data throughput.

Step 4: Training Loop and Pipeline Execution

Once the model and data loader are set up, the training loop orchestrates forward and backward passes across the distributed pipeline. Using a pipeline parallelism engine (e.g., DeepSpeeds PipelineModule), micro-batches are processed in an overlapping manner. For instance:

```
engine, optimizer, _, _ = deepspeed.initialize(
    model=model, model_parameters=model.parameters(), config=ds_config
)

for batch in loader:
    # The engine splits the input into micro-batches internally (e.g., 8 chunks)
    loss = engine(batch['input_ids'], labels=batch['input_ids'])
    engine.backward(loss)
    engine.step()
```

Under the hood, the following operations occur:

- **Forward Pass:** Each pipeline stage processes its chunk of layers. Activations are sent between stages using efficient communication primitives.

- **MoE Dispatch and Expert Parallelism:** At MoE layers, DeepEP handles the dispatch of tokens to experts across the expert group and gathers their outputs, using FP8 for efficient low-precision transfers.

- **Backward Pass:** Using DualPipe scheduling, forward and backward passes are overlapped so that each stage remains busy. Gradients are communicated back through the pipeline.

A simplified pseudocode example for manual pipeline execution (without using a high-level library) might look like this:

```
# On rank corresponding to stage 0:
if pipeline_group_idx == 0:
    out_stage0 = stage0_model(batch) # forward pass through stage 0
    dist.send(out_stage0, dst=next_stage_rank, group=pp_group)
# On intermediate stages:
if 0 < pipeline_group_idx < pipeline_stages - 1:
    activations = torch.empty(..., device=device)
    dist.recv(activations, src=prev_stage_rank, group=pp_group)
    out_stage = stage_model(activations)
    dist.send(out_stage, dst=next_stage_rank, group=pp_group)
# On last stage:
if pipeline_group_idx == pipeline_stages - 1:
    activations = torch.empty(..., device=device)
    dist.recv(activations, src=prev_stage_rank, group=pp_group)
    logits = stage_model(activations)
    loss = loss_fn(logits, labels)
    loss.backward()
    # Gradients flow back through the pipeline in a similar manner.
```

While the above pseudocode simplifies the intricate orchestration, actual implementations rely on libraries like DeepSpeed or Megatron-LM to manage the overlapping and communication efficiently.

Step 5: Checkpointing and Monitoring

Regular checkpointing is essential in such large-scale training. Each process saves its local parameters (including its pipeline and MoE weights) to disk. Frameworks like DeepSpeed offer built-in checkpointing that aggregates these shards into a coherent model state. Additionally, validation metricssuch as perplexity or accuracy on specialized benchmarksare computed periodically using a similar distributed pipeline setup.

Pretraining DeepSeek-R1 is a tour de force of modern distributed training techniques. By combining:

- **MoE layers** for massive capacity with sparse activation,

188

- **Advanced position encoding** and memory-efficient attention (FlashAttention and GQA),

- **Multi-dimensional parallelism** (pipeline parallelism via DualPipe, expert parallelism via DeepEP, and data parallelism), and

- **Efficient data preprocessing** with dynamic splitting and on-the-fly tokenization,

DeepSeek -R1 is trained on 1024 GPUs with nearly perfect hardware utilization, significantly reducing training time and cost. This integrated approach allowed DeepSeek-R1 to achieve remarkable performance on tasks such as mathematical reasoning and code generation, even before subsequent reinforcement learning fine-tuning. For researchers and developers, the DeepSeek-R1 pretraining example provides a blueprint for orchestrating state-of-the-art model training across large-scale clusters, leveraging open-source frameworks and innovative parallelism strategies to push the boundaries of what is computationally feasible.

Chapter 9

Deployment and Inference Optimization for DeepSeek Models

Once large-scale models like DeepSeek's transformers and Mixture-of-Experts (MoE) architectures have been trained, the next challenge is to deploy them efficiently in production. In this chapter, we describe the techniques that enable low-latency inference, scalable serving, and resource-efficient execution. DeepSeek's deployment pipeline combines optimized inference kernels, streaming inference strategies, dynamic expert caching, and distributed inference across heterogeneous hardware to ensure that even models with hundreds of billions of parameters deliver high throughput and sub-second response times.

9.1 Inference Optimization Techniques

DeepSeek s deployment and inference optimizations form a comprehensive strategy for bringing massive models into production. Through highly optimized inference kernels, efficient streaming and distributed inference, intelligent expert caching, and support for heterogeneous hardware, DeepSeek achieves high throughput and low latencyeven for models with hundreds of billions of parameters. These innovations enable real-world applications such as real-time code generation and interactive conversational AI, ensuring that advanced models are not just research prototypes but practical tools deployable across a range of environments.

Optimized Inference Kernels

At inference time, every millisecond counts. DeepSeek employs a suite of highly optimized GPU kernels specifically tuned for modern architectures such as NVIDIA Hopper and Ampere. Key optimizations include:

- **Fused Attention Kernels:** Multi-head attention operations are fused into single, highly efficient GPU kernels. By combining operations that traditionally required multiple separate kernel launches, redundant memory loads are minimized and overhead is reduced.

- **Quantized Matrix Multiplications:** Selected layers leverage reduced precision formats (e.g., FP8 or INT8) for matrix multiplications. This quantization strikes a balance between speed and model accuracy, accelerating computations while keeping error margins minimal.

- **Streamed Key-Value Cache:** In autoregressive decoding, key-value caches are stored in high-speed GPU memory. These caches are updated incrementally and reused across tokens to avoid redundant computations and to ensure that previously computed states remain available.

Together, these optimizations drastically reduce latency and maximize token throughput during inference, even for models with hundreds of billions of parameters.

Efficient Streaming Inference

For real-time applications such as code generation or conversational AI, generating tokens one-by-one with minimal delay is critical. DeepSeeks streaming inference mode is designed with the following principles:

1. **Bulk Prompt Processing:** The model first processes the prompt in a single, bulk forward pass to establish initial key-value caches.

2. **Incremental Forward Passes:** New tokens are generated through a lightweight, incremental forward pass that updates only the most recent cache entries, avoiding full recomputation.

3. **Cached Expert Routing:** For MoE layers, the gating decisions for experts are cached when possible, so that the model avoids recomputing routing for static portions of the prompt.

This design minimizes per-token latency by overlapping communication, computation, and cache updates, ensuring that the system can generate coherent text in real time.

Expert Caching and Lazy Loading

MoE models selectively activate only a subset of experts for each input. DeepSeeks deployment pipeline takes advantage of this sparsity by implementing:

- **Expert Caching:** Frequently accessed experts are kept resident in GPU memory to reduce loading delays. This is particularly beneficial for domains with repetitive content, such as common programming languages.

- **Lazy Expert Loading:** For experts that are rarely used, parameters are loaded from disk or offloaded to slower memory tiers only when required. This dynamic management of expert modules reduces overall memory pressure while ensuring that critical experts are always available.

Through these techniques, DeepSeek efficiently serves large MoE models on clusters with limited GPU memory, balancing responsiveness with resource constraints.

9.2 Distributed Inference Across Multi-GPU Nodes

DeepSeek models often exceed the capacity of a single GPU, necessitating distributed inference across multiple devices. The inference pipeline is designed to prioritize low latency through:

- **Asynchronous Prefetching:** Subsequent layers are preloaded onto neighboring GPUs while the current layer is processing the input. This minimizes wait times during inter-GPU transfers.

- **Overlapped Communication:** Activation transfers between GPUs are scheduled concurrently with local computations, ensuring continuous utilization of compute resources.

- **Adaptive Batch Sizing:** Batch sizes are dynamically adjusted based on live traffic, striking a balance between high throughput and low response times.

These strategies, which resemble training parallelism techniques (like pipeline and tensor parallelism), are carefully tuned for inference so that interactive requests are served with minimal delay.

Support for Heterogeneous Hardware

While DeepSeek models are primarily trained on high-end GPUs, deployment environments are often heterogeneous. DeepSeeks inference stack is designed to run efficiently across various platforms:

- **CUDA and ROCm Backends:** Optimized kernels are provided for both NVIDIA and AMD GPUs, ensuring broad compatibility.

- **CPU Fallback Path:** For smaller models or edge deployments, a highly optimized CPU inference engine is available, leveraging AVX512 or ARM Neon instructions.

- **ONNX Export:** Models can be exported to the ONNX format for use with third-party inference engines, facilitating deployment across cloud services, on-premises clusters, and even mobile devices.

This flexibility allows DeepSeek models to be deployed in diverse environments, from cloud-based APIs to embedded systems.

194

Example: Real-Time Code Generation Service

To illustrate the practical application of these techniques, consider the real-time code generation service provided by DeepSeek-Coder. This service integrates multiple inference optimizations to deliver sub-second responses for code snippets:

1. **Request Handling:** A lightweight REST gateway receives incoming code generation requests. It preprocesses prompts and performs initial tokenization.

2. **Distributed Inference:** The preprocessed request is forwarded to a distributed DeepSeek-Coder instance. This instance leverages pipeline and tensor parallelism to handle autoregressive decoding efficiently.

3. **Expert Caching:** Common programming language experts (e.g., those specializing in Python or JavaScript) are preloaded in GPU memory, ensuring rapid processing without repeated gating computations.

4. **Streaming Generation:** The system processes the prompt in bulk to build key-value caches, then generates tokens incrementally using a streamlined forward pass. Partial responses are streamed back to the user as soon as available.

5. **Post-Processing:** The generated tokens are reassembled into well-formatted code blocks, which are then returned to the user for display or execution.

This multi-stage pipeline ensures that typical code generation requests experience minimal latency, even when the underlying model contains hundreds of billions of parameters.

9.3 Efficient Model Quantization

Efficient model quantization is a critical optimization for deploying large language models like DeepSeek, as it can dramatically accelerate inference and reduce memory usage. By reducing the numerical precision of weights and activations, quantization leverages lower-bit arithmetic to compress models without a significant drop in accuracy. In DeepSeek models, both FP8 (8-bit floating point) and INT4 (4-bit integer) quantization play important roles. This section explores how these methods are applied both during training through quantization-aware training (QAT) and after training via post-training quantization (PTQ)and discusses the trade-offs between model accuracy and efficiency.

Role of FP8 and INT4 Quantization

Lowering the numerical precision of model parameters and activations can lead to considerable reductions in memory footprint and computational cost:

- **FP8 Precision (E4M3/E5M2):** This format uses only 8 bits to represent numbers (with 1 sign bit, 4 or 5 exponent bits, and 2 or 3 mantissa bits). DeepSeeks FP8 mixed-precision framework employs FP8 arithmetic for operations such as matrix multiplications and caching activations. The careful selection of FP8 operationswhile maintaining critical computations (e.g., attention and normalization) in higher precision like BF16 or FP32ensures both speed and numerical stability.

- **INT4 Quantization:** Typically used for weight-only quantization, INT4 reduces model weights to 4-bit fixed-point integers. This can compress the weight storage by up to 8 compared to FP32, enabling the deployment of massive models on hardware with limited memory. Deployment frameworks such as TensorRT-LLM have demonstrated the practical feasibility of INT4 quantized checkpoints with minimal accuracy loss.

The benefits of these techniques are twofold:

- **Latency and Throughput Improvements:** Smaller models mean faster data movement and more efficient use of cache, often the limiting factor in inference speed. On NVIDIA H100 GPUs, FP8 kernels can achieve up to 3 throughput improvements over FP16 or BF16, while INT4 weight quantization can unlock significant speedups by enabling accelerated 4-bit Tensor Core operations.

- **Reduced Memory Footprint:** A lower-bit representation directly translates to lower GPU VRAM usage. This reduction is particularly important when serving very large models or when deploying on resource-constrained devices.

Quantization-Aware Training (QAT) in PyTorch

Quantization-aware training (QAT) simulates the effects of quantization during training, allowing the model to adapt to lower precision and maintain higher accuracy. PyTorch provides native support for QAT via fake quantization modules. Below is an example of how one might apply QAT to a DeepSeek transformer block:

```
import torch
import torch.quantization as tq

# Assume 'model' is an instance of a DeepSeek transformer block
model.eval() # Set the model to evaluation mode for static quantization preparation
# Define a QAT configuration (here using the 'fbgemm' backend)
qat_config = tq.get_default_qat_qconfig('fbgemm')
model.qconfig = qat_config

# Prepare the model for quantization-aware training by inserting fake quantization
    modules
tq.prepare_qat(model, inplace=True)

# Fine-tune the model for a few epochs to adapt to quantization
optimizer = torch.optim.Adam(model.parameters(), lr=1e-5)
for epoch in range(2):
    for inputs, targets in train_loader:
        optimizer.zero_grad()
        outputs = model(inputs)
        loss = criterion(outputs, targets)
        loss.backward()
        optimizer.step()

# Convert the model to a fully quantized version (e.g., with INT8 weights)
model_int8 = tq.convert(model.eval(), inplace=False)
```

In this workflow, the model is initially prepared for QAT, then fine-tuned so that the network learns to mitigate quantization errors. Once the QAT phase is complete, the model is converted to a quantized version suitable for efficient inference.

Post-Training Quantization (PTQ) in PyTorch

As an alternative to QAT, post-training quantization (PTQ) is a one-shot approach applied to a pre-trained model. PTQ uses calibration data to determine optimal scaling factors for weights and activations. PyTorchs `torch.quantization.quantize_dynamic` function is commonly used to perform dynamic quantization on linear layers. Here is an example of static PTQ for a DeepSeek model:

197

```
import torch.quantization as tq

# Set the model to evaluation mode and assign a static quantization configuration
model.eval()
model.qconfig = tq.default_static_qconfig

# Prepare the model for quantization (inserting observers to collect statistics)
tq.prepare(model, inplace=True)

# Calibrate the model using a representative calibration dataset
with torch.no_grad():
    for inputs, _ in calibration_loader:
        _ = model(inputs)

# Convert the model to its quantized form, which quantizes weights to INT8
model_int8 = tq.convert(model, inplace=False)
```

PTQ is simpler to apply since it requires no additional training, but it often results in a slightly higher accuracy degradation compared to QAT. Recent advances like SmoothQuant and GPTQ have been proposed to minimize these losses further.

Accuracy vs. Efficiency Trade-Offs

Both QAT and PTQ offer significant efficiency gains at the expense of some accuracy. QAT generally preserves more of the original model accuracy by simulating quantization during training, whereas PTQ is easier to apply but may incur a larger accuracy drop. The choice of quantization schemewhether FP8 for mixed precision or INT4 for weight-only quantizationshould be based on the specific requirements of your application. The goal is to choose the lowest precision that still maintains acceptable accuracy while maximizing throughput and reducing memory usage.

Efficient model quantization, through techniques like FP8 and INT4, is key to accelerating inference and reducing the memory footprint of DeepSeek models. By employing QAT or PTQ, practitioners can strike a balance between model accuracy and efficiency, enabling the deployment of massive models on a wide range of hardware platforms. The examples provided illustrate practical ways to integrate quantization into a PyTorch workflow, ensuring that large models remain both performant and resource-efficient in production.

9.4 Optimized Serving with TensorRT and FasterTransformer

To achieve low-latency inference and fully leverage GPU hardware, DeepSeek models can be deployed using specialized inference frameworks such as **NVIDIA TensorRT** and **FasterTransformer**. These frameworks provide highly optimized CUDA kernels, support for lower precision (e.g., INT8, FP8), and advanced multi-threading capabilities, enabling rapid, scalable inference for even the most complex models.

Hardware-Optimized Inference Frameworks

NVIDIA TensorRT is a deep learning inference SDK that transforms neural network models into highly optimized runtime engines for NVIDIA GPUs. Its main features include:

- **Layer and Tensor Fusion:** Combining multiple operations into a single kernel to reduce memory bandwidth usage.

- **Automatic Mixed Precision:** Automatically optimizing operations for FP16 or INT8, with calibration routines to maintain accuracy.

- **Engine Builder:** Generating a serialized engine tailored to the target hardware, which can be deployed in production.

FasterTransformer is an open-source library providing C++/CUDA implementations of transformer blocks specifically designed for high-speed inference. It offers:

- Highly optimized multi-head attention, layer normalization, and decoding routines.

- Support for custom optimizations such as fused attention kernels and quantized computations.

- Integration with frameworks like Hugging Face Transformers or TensorRT-LLM to directly support large language models.

199

Both frameworks can leverage **Tensor Cores** for FP16/FP8 matrix multiplications and custom kernels (e.g., for fused Multi-Head Attention) and can utilize batching and stream-based execution to further accelerate inference.

Converting DeepSeek Models to TensorRT

Converting a DeepSeek PyTorch model to TensorRT typically involves exporting the model to ONNX and then using TensorRTs builder to create an optimized engine. The process can be summarized as follows:

1. **Export to ONNX:** Use `torch.onnx.export` on the models `forward` method, providing dummy inputs with an appropriate sequence length. Custom operations (like MLA) may require custom ONNX operators or the use of TensorRT-LLM which supports certain LLM architectures natively.

2. **Build the TensorRT Engine:** Use the `trtexec` CLI or the Python API to load the ONNX model and build an engine with desired optimizations such as FP16 or INT8 precision.

For example, the following Python code snippet demonstrates building a TensorRT engine with FP16 precision:

```
import tensorrt as trt

onnx_model = "deepseek.onnx"
engine_file = "deepseek.plan"
logger = trt.Logger(trt.Logger.INFO)
builder = trt.Builder(logger)
network = builder.create_network(1 << int(trt.NetworkDefinitionCreationFlag.
    EXPLICIT_BATCH))
parser = trt.OnnxParser(network, logger)
with open(onnx_model, "rb") as f:
    parser.parse(f.read())

# Configure builder settings
config = builder.create_builder_config()
config.max_workspace_size = 1 << 30 # 1GB workspace
config.set_flag(trt.BuilderFlag.FP16)
# Optionally, enable INT8 calibration:
# config.set_flag(trt.BuilderFlag.INT8)
# config.int8_calibrator = MyCalibrator()

# Build and serialize the engine
engine = builder.build_engine(network, config)
with open(engine_file, "wb") as f:
    f.write(engine.serialize())
```

TensorRT-LLM simplifies this process further by providing scripts that directly convert DeepSeek-V2/V3 models into optimized engines with support for FP8 and INT4 quantization.

Verification and Deployment

Once the TensorRT engine is built, it can be deployed using either C++ or Python. For example, the following Python code demonstrates running inference on the engine:

```python
import numpy as np
import pycuda.driver as cuda
import pycuda.autoinit

# Load the engine and create an execution context
runtime = trt.Runtime(logger)
with open("deepseek.plan", "rb") as f:
    engine = runtime.deserialize_cuda_engine(f.read())
context = engine.create_execution_context()

# Prepare input and output buffers
input_shape = engine.get_binding_shape(0)
output_shape = engine.get_binding_shape(1)
d_input = cuda.mem_alloc(np.prod(input_shape) * np.float16().nbytes)
d_output = cuda.mem_alloc(np.prod(output_shape) * np.float16().nbytes)

# Prepare a dummy input (e.g., token IDs) and execute inference
host_input = np.random.randint(0, 50257, size=input_shape, dtype=np.int32)
cuda.memcpy_htod(d_input, host_input)
context.execute_v2(bindings=[int(d_input), int(d_output)])
host_output = np.empty(output_shape, dtype=np.float16)
cuda.memcpy_dtoh(host_output, d_output)
print("Next token logits:", host_output)
```

This skeleton can be integrated into a production serving pipeline that continuously generates tokens in a loop for autoregressive tasks.

CUDA-based Optimizations with FasterTransformer

For even higher performance, FasterTransformer offers its own highly optimized transformer implementations. Using FasterTransformer, one typically:

- Converts model weights into FasterTransformers internal format (often using provided conversion scripts).

- Uses the FasterTransformer GPT interface to perform fast decoding with optimized multi-head attention and layer norm operations.

201

- Leverages GPU-specific optimizations, including half-precision computations and fused operations.

A brief example using FasterTransformers PyTorch integration might look like
this:

```
from transformers import AutoTokenizer
from faster_transformer import FasterTransformerGPT

tokenizer = AutoTokenizer.from_pretrained("deepseek-v3")
ft_model = FasterTransformerGPT.from_pretrained("deepseek-v3",
               tensor_para_size=1, pipeline_para_size=1)
input_ids = tokenizer("Hello, DeepSeek!", return_tensors="pt").input_ids
output = ft_model.generate(input_ids, max_new_tokens=50, do_sample=False)
print(tokenizer.decode(output[0]))
```

This example illustrates how FasterTransformer can be employed for rapid text
generation, leveraging its custom CUDA kernels and optimized data flows.

By converting DeepSeek models to optimized inference engines using
NVIDIA TensorRT or FasterTransformer, one can achieve extremely low
latency and high throughput. These frameworks exploit advanced GPU
featuressuch as Tensor Cores, fused operations, and efficient quantizationto
accelerate the forward pass. The conversion process typically involves
exporting the model to ONNX, building a tailored engine with precision
flags, and verifying performance through test inference. Such optimizations
are essential for serving large-scale models in production, ensuring that
real-time applications, like interactive code generation or conversational AI,
operate at peak efficiency.

9.5 Distributed Inference Scaling

Deploying large DeepSeek models, which often consist of tens or hundreds of
billions of parameters (especially in MoE configurations), requires distributing inference across multiple GPUs or even across multiple nodes. This section outlines strategies for achieving scalable, low-latency inference by combining multi-GPU and multi-node techniques, load balancing for concurrent
requests, and specialized expert-parallel methods for MoE layers. We also provide an example using PyTorch and DeepSpeeds Inference Engine to illustrate
multi-GPU serving.

Multi-GPU Inference Techniques

When the model size or throughput requirements exceed the capacity of a single GPU, various forms of parallelism are employed:

- **Tensor Parallelism (TP):** In tensor parallelism, the models weight matrices (e.g., those in linear layers) are split across multiple GPUs. Each GPU computes a portion of the overall operation, and the results are combined to form the final output. Frameworks such as DeepSpeed-Inference and Megatron-LM provide transparent TP, where the degree of parallelism (e.g., 2-way or 4-way) is chosen based on available hardware and memory constraints.

- **Pipeline Parallelism (PP):** Pipeline parallelism divides the models layers into sequential stages that reside on different GPUs. Although sequential processing can introduce idle bubbles due to autoregressive dependencies, these can be mitigated by micro-batching or combining with TP to keep all stages busy.

- **Sequence Parallelism:** This approach splits the input sequence itself across devices and is more commonly used during training for very long sequences. For inference, its utility is more limited compared to TP or PP.

- **Expert Parallelism for MoE:** In Mixture-of-Experts layers, only a few experts are activated per token. With expert parallelism, the experts are partitioned across GPUs so that each device only hosts a subset of experts. For instance, if a MoE layer has 128 experts and the system uses 8 GPUs, each GPU might host 16 experts. During inference, the gating network selects the top-k experts for each token, and the token representations are routed to the GPUs holding those experts.

In many deployments, TP and PP are combined (e.g., 2-way TP with 2-stage PP to use 4 GPUs) to maximize resource utilization. Expert parallelism is handled by specialized libraries (such as FastMoE or custom router implementations) that manage the dynamic routing of tokens to experts.

Multi-Node Inference and Load Balancing

For models that cannot be contained on a single server, multi-node inference becomes essential. Two primary strategies are used:

- **Model Parallel Inference:** The model is partitioned across nodes using model parallelism techniques (e.g., TP and PP) with high-speed interconnects such as NVIDIA NCCL over InfiniBand.

- **Data Parallel Inference:** Separate instances of the model are run on different nodes, and a load balancer distributes incoming requests among these instances to optimize throughput and response time.

When serving multiple concurrent requests, an external load balancer ensures that work is evenly distributed across GPUs or nodes. This is especially important for MoE models where some experts may be more popular than others. DeepSeek-V3 employs an auxiliary-loss-free load balancing strategy during training to encourage even expert utilization. At inference, dynamic routing can further help avoid overloading any single GPU.

Example: Multi-GPU Inference with DeepSpeed

The following example demonstrates how to deploy a DeepSeek model using DeepSpeeds Inference Engine with tensor parallelism across multiple GPUs:

```
import torch
import deepspeed
from transformers import AutoModelForCausalLM, AutoTokenizer

model_name = "deepseek-v3"
tokenizer = AutoTokenizer.from_pretrained(model_name)
model = AutoModelForCausalLM.from_pretrained(model_name, torch_dtype=torch.float16
    )

# Move the model to CPU first to avoid GPU memory overflow before partitioning
model.to('cpu')

# Initialize DeepSpeed Inference Engine with 4-way tensor parallelism
ds_engine = deepspeed.init_inference(
    model,
    mp_size=4, # Tensor parallelism: split model across 4 GPUs
    dtype=torch.half,
    replace_with_kernel_inject=True
)
model = ds_engine.module # The model is now partitioned and optimized
```

```
# Prepare input and generate text
input_text = "DeepSeek models achieve remarkable efficiency through"
inputs = tokenizer(input_text, return_tensors='pt').to(0) # Send to GPU 0
outputs = model.generate(**inputs, max_new_tokens=40, do_sample=False)
print(tokenizer.decode(outputs[0]))
```

In this script, DeepSpeed partitions the model across 4 GPUs, injecting optimized kernels (e.g., fused attention operations) for accelerated inference. The DeepSpeed Inference Engine automatically manages cross-GPU communication, ensuring that the generated tokens are assembled correctly.

For multi-node inference, the script can be launched with a multi-node launcher (such as `torchrun` or DeepSpeeds CLI) using environment variables like `WORLD_SIZE` to coordinate processes across nodes.

Scaling inference for DeepSeek models requires a careful blend of model parallelism techniques and robust load balancing. By employing tensor and pipeline parallelism (and expert parallelism for MoE layers), distributed inference can meet both latency and memory constraints across multiple GPUs and nodes. Frameworks like DeepSpeed simplify this process by automating the partitioning and optimized communication, enabling the deployment of state-of-the-art models even in high-throughput, low-latency production environments.

9.6 Streaming and Low-Latency Techniques

Real-time applications such as live chat and interactive assistants demand extremely low latency during inference. To meet these requirements, DeepSeeks deployment pipeline incorporates several advanced strategies that reduce waiting time for users while maintaining high throughput under heavy load. In this section, we detail methods including **speculative decoding**, **prefix caching**, **continuous batching**, and **parallel sampling**each designed to accelerate token generation without compromising output quality.

Speculative Decoding

Speculative decoding is an effective method to speed up autoregressive generation by leveraging a smaller, faster *draft model* to propose multiple tokens in advance. The process involves:

- Running a lightweight draft model (e.g., a 1B parameter distilled version) that rapidly generates a short sequence of tokens.

- Conditioning the full DeepSeek model on the first token and verifying if its predictions align with the drafts proposal.

- Accepting the entire block of tokens if they match, or otherwise reverting to the DeepSeek models output at the point of divergence.

This method can nearly double the speed of token generation when the draft model frequently yields valid proposals. A simplified pseudocode outline is provided below:

```
# Initialize models
draft_model = AutoModelForCausalLM.from_pretrained("smaller_model")
main_model = AutoModelForCausalLM.from_pretrained(" DeepSeek -v3")

input_ids = tokenizer(prompt, return_tensors='pt').input_ids

# Obtain initial logits from the main model
outputs = main_model(input_ids)

while not finished:
    # Draft model generates N tokens quickly
    draft_tokens = []
    for _ in range(N):
        draft_logits = draft_model(input_ids)
        draft_next = sample_from_logits(draft_logits)
        draft_tokens.append(draft_next)
        input_ids = torch.cat([input_ids, draft_next], dim=-1)

    # Main model verifies the draft in one forward pass
    outputs = main_model(input_ids)
    match_len = compute_match(outputs.logits, draft_tokens)

    # Accept the matching tokens and adjust input_ids accordingly
    result.extend(draft_tokens[:match_len])
    if match_len < len(draft_tokens):
        true_token = torch.argmax(outputs.logits[..., -1, :], dim=-1)
        input_ids = torch.cat([input_ids[:-len(draft_tokens)], true_token], dim=-1)
        result.append(true_token)
```

Prefix Caching and Continuous Batching

Prefix caching is particularly beneficial when multiple inference requests share a common initial prompt. By computing the key-value (KV) cache for this shared prefix only once and reusing it across requests, the system avoids redundant computation and accelerates subsequent decoding. Modern systems

206

such as vLLM implement this by maintaining a cache mapping of prefixes to KV states, which is periodically pruned based on usage.

In tandem, **continuous batching** (or dynamic batching) aggregates incoming requests in short time windows (e.g., every 10 ms) to form a batch. This technique minimizes latency by rapidly grouping pending requests, enabling the model to process several sequences in parallel without waiting for a large, fixed batch size. Continuous batching ensures that even with variable arrival rates, the GPU remains fully utilized.

Parallel Sampling and Token Merging

To further reduce latency, parallel sampling techniques allow the system to generate multiple candidate tokens simultaneously. For instance, by sampling the top-k candidates in parallel, the model can quickly decide whether to accept a group of tokens or re-sample when confidence is high. This method is akin to speculative decoding, but without employing a separate draft model, instead relying on vectorized operations on the GPU. The following example demonstrates a simple approach to parallel sampling:

```
# Compute logits for the next token
logits = model(input_ids).logits[:, -1, :] # shape: (batch, vocab)
probs = torch.softmax(logits, dim=-1)
topk_prob, topk_idx = torch.topk(probs, k=3, dim=-1) # Top-3 candidates

# Create multiple continuations for each candidate
branches = []
for i in range(topk_idx.size(1)):
    new_input = torch.cat([input_ids, topk_idx[:, i].unsqueeze(-1)], dim=-1)
    branches.append(new_input)

# Process branches in parallel to decide the best continuation
```

Such parallel sampling can be integrated with token merging strategies, where multiple tokens are generated in a single forward pass by unrolling the transformer several steps, thereby reducing the number of expensive inference calls.

In summary, DeepSeeks streaming and low-latency techniques are designed to minimize the delay in generating tokens for real-time applications. By:

- Leveraging speculative decoding to potentially accept multiple tokens per forward pass,

- Caching common prefixes to avoid redundant computations,

- Continuously batching incoming requests to maximize GPU utilization, and

- Employing parallel sampling strategies to reduce tail latency,

the inference pipeline achieves both high throughput and low per-token latency. These optimizations ensure that interactive applications, such as live chat or code generation, can deliver prompt and coherent responses even under heavy load.

9.7 Efficient Deployment on Cloud and Edge Devices

Deploying DeepSeek models into production requires a balance of raw inference speed, robust performance, and scalability across various hardware platforms. Whether running on cloud GPU servers or on resource-constrained edge devices, careful optimization and packaging are key. In this section, we describe best practices for containerizing and serving DeepSeek models using industry-standard frameworks such as NVIDIA Triton Inference Server and ONNX Runtime, and we discuss optimizations tailored for both cloud and edge deployments.

Containerized Model Serving with Triton and ONNX Runtime

Leveraging a standardized inference server simplifies deployment and helps manage critical tasks like dynamic batching, model versioning, and scaling. Two popular options are:

- **NVIDIA Triton Inference Server:** This server supports multiple frameworks (e.g., PyTorch, TensorRT, ONNX) within a single deployment. With Triton, you can:
  - Convert DeepSeek models to an ONNX or TensorRT format.
  - Organize models in a standardized repository structure with configuration files to set parameters such as maximum batch size, dynamic batching policies, and optimization profiles for different sequence lengths.

208

- Handle HTTP/gRPC requests efficiently, manage model ensembles (for example, combining a preprocessing module with the core model), and dynamically scale resources based on traffic.

- **ONNX Runtime (ORT):** As a cross-platform inference engine, ORT offers robust support on CPUs, GPUs, and even in browser environments via WebAssembly. With specialized transformer optimizations (such as graph fusion and mixed precision), ORT can run DeepSeek models significantly faster than PyTorch. This makes it an excellent choice for deployments that require portability or need to run on varied hardware.

For example, to deploy a DeepSeek model with Triton, you would package your model in a repository as follows:

```
model_repository/deepseek/1/model.onnx
model_repository/deepseek/config.pbtxt
```

A typical `config.pbtxt` might be:

```
name: "deepseek"
platform: "onnxruntime_onnx" # or "tensorrt_plan" for TensorRT engines
max_batch_size: 8
input [
  {
    name: "input_ids"
    data_type: TYPE_INT32
    dims: [ -1 ] # dynamic sequence length
  }
]
output [
  {
    name: "logits"
    data_type: TYPE_FP32
    dims: [ -1, $VOCAB_SIZE ]
  }
]
instance_group [
  {
    kind: KIND_GPU
    count: 1
    gpus: [ 0 ]
  }
]
dynamic_batching { max_queue_delay_microseconds: 10000 }
```

Triton, when deployed via Docker (e.g., from `nvcr.io/nvidia/tritonserver`), can then handle incoming requests and dynamically manage resources based on load.

209

Cloud GPU Serving Optimizations

For deployments on cloud GPUs (such as AWS EC2, Azure, or GCP), the following optimizations are essential:

- **Mixed Precision:** Utilizing FP16 or BF16 for weights and computations allows you to double throughput by leveraging Tensor Cores.

- **Autoscaling:** Deploy your model on a platform (such as Kubernetes) that automatically scales the number of serving replicas based on demand.

- **Resource Pinning and Affinity:** Ensuring that GPUs are dedicated to your inference process and that CPU threads are pinned to specific cores minimizes context switching and maximizes performance.

- **Model Compression for Transit:** Use efficient storage formats (e.g., safetensors in half precision) to reduce model deployment times and overhead.

For MoE models, additional strategies such as dedicated expert serving frameworks can be employed, wherein the experts are distributed and managed across nodes to balance load and reduce latency.

Edge Deployment for Resource-Constrained Environments

When deploying on edge devices (smartphones, Raspberry Pi, Jetson Nano, etc.), the primary concerns are low power consumption and limited memory:

- **Optimized Inference Engines:** Use ONNX Runtime with NNAPI (Android) or CoreML (Apple) to run models on mobile neural accelerators.

- **Model Distillation and Quantization:** Deploy smaller, distilled versions of DeepSeek (e.g., DeepSeek-R1-distill-1.5B) in INT8 or lower precision to fit within the limited memory of edge devices.

- **Hardware Acceleration:** Exploit any available on-device hardware acceleration, whether via DSPs, NPUs, or GPUs.

For example, using ONNX Runtime on a Raspberry Pi might involve:

```
import onnxruntime as ort
import numpy as np

sess_options = ort.SessionOptions()
sess_options.intra_op_num_threads = 1
session = ort.InferenceSession("deepseek_quant.onnx", sess_options)
input_ids = np.array([[101, 2023, 2003, 1037, ...]], dtype=np.int64)
outputs = session.run(["logits"], {"input_ids": input_ids})
print("Logits:", outputs[0])
```

If the edge device includes a small GPU (e.g., NVIDIA Jetson), TensorRT engines can be deployed similarly.

Best Practices Summary

- **Cloud Deployments:** Containerize your model using Triton or a custom server with DeepSpeed Inference. Optimize throughput with mixed precision, dynamic batching, and autoscaling. Turnkey solutions such as HuggingFaces TGI or vLLM can simplify this process.

- **Edge Deployments:** Focus on minimizing model size through distillation, quantization, and pruning. Use ONNX Runtime or TensorFlow Lite to ensure portability, and leverage available hardware accelerators for efficient inference.

- **General Considerations:** Monitor latency and memory usage to avoid overloading the system. Implement fallbacks (such as a smaller model) if the primary model is under heavy load, ensuring a robust, scalable serving system.

By following these strategies, developers can deploy DeepSeek models in production with confidence, ensuring they meet the necessary latency and throughput requirements whether it's a powerful cloud server or a small edge device. The key is to combine model optimizations (quantization, efficient caching) with system-level optimizations (container orchestration, hardware acceleration) to achieve end-to-end efficiency.

References

[1] DeepSeek. "DeepSeek LLM: Open Sourcing a Family of High-Performance Language Models." arXiv preprint arXiv:2401.14196v2, 2024.

[2] DeepSeek. " DeepSeek MoE: Scaling Mixture of Experts Language Models Efficiently to 67B Active Parameters." arXiv preprint arXiv:2406.11931v1, 2024.

[3] DeepSeek. " DeepSeek -V2: Enhancing LLM Reasoning Abilities through Process Supervision and Stepwise Training." arXiv preprint arXiv:2412.19437v2, 2024.

[4] DeepSeek. " DeepSeek -R1: Pushing Reasoning to New Heights with Reinforcement Learning and Grouped Policy Optimization." arXiv preprint arXiv:2501.12948v1, 2025.

[5] Vaswani, A., Shazeer, N., Parmar, N., et al. "Attention Is All You Need." Advances in Neural Information Processing Systems (NeurIPS), 2017.

[6] Shazeer, N., Mirhoseini, A., Maziarz, K., et al. "Outrageously Large Neural Networks: The Sparsely-Gated Mixture-of-Experts Layer." arXiv preprint arXiv:1701.06538, 2017.

[7] Cobbe, K., Kosaraju, V., Bavarian, M., et al. "GSM8K: A Dataset for Grade School Math Word Problems." arXiv preprint arXiv:2109.05066, 2021.

[8] Hendrycks, D., Burns, C., Basart, S., et al. "Measuring Massive Multitask Language Understanding." arXiv preprint arXiv:2009.03300, 2020.

[9] Chen, M., Tworek, J., Jun, H., et al. "Evaluating Large Language Models Trained on Code." arXiv preprint arXiv:2107.03374, 2021.

[10] Open LLM Leaderboard. "Open LLM Leaderboard: Benchmarking Open Language Models." Available at: https://huggingface.co/spaces/HuggingFaceH4/open_llm_leaderboard, accessed 2025.

[11] Liang, P., et al. "HELM: Holistic Evaluation of Language Models." Stanford Center for Research on Foundation Models, 2022.

[12] Zhang, P., Roller, S., Goyal, N., et al. "OPT: Open Pre-trained Transformer Language Models." arXiv preprint arXiv:2205.01068, 2022.

[13] Brown, T., Mann, B., Ryder, N., et al. "Language Models are Few-Shot Learners." Advances in Neural Information Processing Systems (NeurIPS), 2020.

[14] DeepSeek GitHub Organization. Available at: https://github.com/deepseek-ai, accessed 2025.

[15] DeepEP: Expert Parallel Communication Library. Available at: https://github.com/deepseek-ai/DeepEP, accessed 2025.

[16] DualPipe: Bidirectional Pipeline Parallelism. Available at: https://github.com/deepseek-ai/DualPipe, accessed 2025.

[17] 3FS: Distributed File System for AI Training Data. Available at: https://github.com/deepseek-ai/3FS, accessed 2025.

[18] FlashMLA: Efficient Multi-Layer Attention. Available at: https://github.com/deepseek-ai/FlashMLA, accessed 2025.

[19] NVIDIA TensorRT. Available at: https://developer.nvidia.com/tensorrt, accessed 2025.

[20] FasterTransformer GitHub Repository. Available at: https://github.com/NVIDIA/FasterTransformer, accessed 2025.

[21] DeepSpeed Inference Documentation. Available at: https://www.deepspeed.ai/inference/, accessed 2025.

[22] NVIDIA Triton Inference Server Documentation. Available at: https://developer.nvidia.com/nvidia-triton-inference-server, accessed 2025.

[23] ONNX Runtime Documentation. Available at: https://onnxruntime.ai, accessed 2025.

[24] Chen, T., Leng, C., Li, Y., et al. "Speculative Decoding for Large Lan-

guage Models." arXiv preprint arXiv:2302.01318, 2023.

[25] vLLM Project. "vLLM: A High-Throughput Serving System for LLM Inference." Available at: https://github.com/vllm-project/vllm, accessed 2025.

[26] Microsoft Olive. Available at: https://github.com/microsoft/Olive, accessed 2025.

Acknowledgement

The author would like to explicitly state that this work is entirely independent and has no affiliation with DeepSeek or its parent organizations. All content within this book is derived from publicly available sources, including DeepSeeks published papers, open-source code repositories, public benchmark results, and additional materials accessible through the internet. Every effort has been made to ensure accuracy, but this book does not represent the views or endorsements of DeepSeek or its team.

The author wishes to extend deep appreciation to the DeepSeek team for their remarkable contribution to the open-source AI community. By releasing both high-performance models and detailed technical documentation, DeepSeek has significantly advanced the accessibility of cutting-edge language model research. Their commitment to transparency and collaboration sets a high standard for the future of responsible AI development.

Despite best efforts, errors or omissions may exist in this book. The author welcomes feedback and corrections from readers, and encourages anyone who identifies inaccuracies or areas needing improvement to reach out. Together, we can contribute to a richer and more accurate understanding of open-source language model development.